PREFACE.

THE old maxim, *cuicunque in arte suâ perito credendum est,* being in some danger, from our reviewers and amateurs having determined, *coute qui coute,* to become the instructors of the public in matters of architecture, I have thrown together the few hints contained in the following pages, in the hope that the existence of so sound a maxim may be a little longer protracted. I may, perhaps, be thought guilty of great presumption in not leaving the task I have undertaken to some other professor more capable of instructing the parties for whose benefit the work is intended; having, however, waited in vain for the appearance of some such person, I resolved that, however feebly I might perform it, I would no longer refrain from the attempt.

The reviews and magazines are all in violent commotion, because architects seem to have some awkward misgivings on the competency of their writers as judges of art—nay, more; one critic, whose essays I shall more especially notice, appears to think that the

architect is jealous of them, and has, moreover, discovered that "their antipathy towards amateurs extends
only to living ones, since praise is ungrudgingly bestowed
on those who have quitted the stage ; on a Wotton,
and an Evelyn, an Aldrich, a Burrowes, a Clarke, a
Burlington, a Walpole, and a Hope." Of the two last
and the two first, who, by the way, do not present very
suitable qualifications for comparison, it is merely to
be observed, that they were more theoretically than
practically versed in the art, though on the two last I
have some doubts—perhaps on the last, none.   But
Aldrich, Burrowes, Clark, and Burlington, were
actually practical amateurs, and beyond that, men of
profound learning, who bequeathed to their posterity
such specimens of architecture as to give the world
assurance they were something more than prattlers on
art; indeed, with the exception of Aldrich, among the
four, I am not aware that either has left any other me-
morial of his name, as connected with architecture,
than his buildings.   Aldriches and Burlingtons are
not, however, produced every day, more than Addi-
sons or Howards.   When they do appear they will be
hailed by the profession as welcome intruders ; such are
always serviceable to the profession, from the taste and
tone they infuse into their own class.   The reviewers
and amateurs must, therefore, excuse the profession
for doubting their qualifications, and trying the *quan-*

ELEMENTS

OF

ARCHITECTURAL CRITICISM

FOR THE USE OF

STUDENTS, AMATEURS, AND REVIEWERS.

BY

JOSEPH GWILT,

AUTHOR OF A TRANSLATION OF VITRUVIUS, &c., &c, &c.

——————— inquirendo scribendoque talia consolemur otium nostrum, quæ futura usui bonæ mentis juvenibus arbitramur, nobis certe sunt Voluptati.—*Quintilian.*

LONDON:

JOHN WILLIAMS,

LIBRARY OF FINE ARTS, CHARLES STREET, SOHO SQUARE.

M. DCCC. XXXVII.

tum valeat of their criticism, until, by their works, they are better known.   To suppose that among the highly educated nobility and gentry of these realms, members of those classes are not to be found who have not the aptitude and ability to make themselves acquainted with the art, is too absurd for a moment's consideration ; but the fact is, that the all-absorbing influence of party and politics, in this country, abstracts them too much from all other pursuits ; hence so few among them are found capable of bestowing their patronage with judgment and utility to the public, and hence such buildings as that recently erected at Charing Cross.

From many concurrent causes the French School of Architecture has for many years exhibited a high degree of excellence, and in the present day must be considered as holding the highest rank in Europe. As one of the causes, may be fairly assigned the strict justice that has usually followed in all their *concurrences* or competitions ; the selection of the best design being usually made by artists themselves. Another cause is easily traced in the habits of the people, which allow one large mass of building to be inhabited by many tenants ; hence the construction of a series of apparent palaces instead of a row of insignificant houses. Another cause is, the severity with which the early studies of a French architect are con-

ducted, and the hopelessness of succeeding by patronage without a regular education to the art. All
these things, if they do not always produce greatness,
yet raise art above mediocrity. Much has been
written and said upon the recent decision upon the
designs for the new Houses of Parliament. One
reviewer has compared it to the judgment of Paris,
and seems vexed that the profession was not satisfied
with the dictum of the Commissioners : but he has
forgotten that there is another judgment recorded in
ancient fabulous history, in which Apollo was a principal performer, but which I will not name, though the
profession have likened it to the decision in question.
It is not here to be understood that I allude in the
remotest manner to the selection of Mr. Barry's beautiful designs; but of its three successful companions,
without intending any reflection on them or their
authors, or on the parties who selected them, it is
beyond all question certain, that, as compared with
very many of the unsuccessful ones, the decision was
unjust, because erroneous. If the selection had been
left to the competitors themselves, each having a
number of votes equal to the number of premiums,
justice would have been done ; and I think it more
than probable that Mr. Barry would have occupied
the station he now holds. Not myself concerned
in the competition, nor knowing one half of the

competitors, my judgment may, perhaps, pass for something on this head. I could not avoid mentioning
this subject here, because the dissatisfaction of the
architects has been made the medium of treating the
profession rather unfairly, in the last number of an
extensively circulated and highly respectable periodical,
in whose sentiments, as to propriety and preference of
the Italian style, it will be seen I concur.

I have, in the following work, fearlessly expressed
my opinion on the present German School of Architecture; indeed, I do not hesitate to declare that as
one of my leading motives in writing the following
sheets. I have done so to disabuse, if I am right,
the public, but more especially the architectural
student, being of opinion that though ultimately the
structures at Berlin and Munich, which are the theme
of much admiration, and proposed as models for us by
the reviewer in the Foreign Quarterly, will, as all
fashionable art does, shortly find their level, yet a
protest is due from those who may fairly be presumed
to know more about the matter than the reviewer,
and to prevent the unwary being led astray. At the
same time, it must not be supposed that I am insensible to the talents of the artists I have criticised, nor
desirous of diminishing, if it were in the power of so
humble an individual as myself, their deserved reputation. Their works are the property of the public,

and if I am wrong in my judgment, I must be content
to bear the disgrace of an attempt to detract from
their merits.   My feeling is, they have trusted too
much to decoration, and too little to general forms ;
that, in the endeavour to unite the Grecian style,
strictly so called, with the arrangements of the Italian
school, they have produced a style which partakes of
the beauties of neither, because the one is destructive
of the other.   That this union will be ever tastefully
obtained I much doubt, but I may be wrong ; up to
this period the problem is not solved.   The attempt
induced the appearance of manner, whose absence is
necessary before taste can exist: for this is neither
arbitrary nor founded on fantastic conventions, nor to
be acquired except by that natural endowment and
cultivation of the mind, which generates the nicest
and most exact discernment.   There has existed in this
country of late, a seeming desire to underrate the architectural talent which it has produced ; looking, however, to what has been actually executed in London, as
well as the provinces, I do not think this fair.   Where
the opportunities have been afforded, except in some
of the Government buildings, an average example of
talent has been elicited ; and if the age has not produced such specimens as graced the beginning of the
last century, it must be confessed that a mighty stride
has been made since the miserable taste of the

Adamses was the object of unbounded patronage by the fashionable world. Still, if the art were even lower than those who revile the state of it describe it to be, is it to be attributed to the architect? Is there nothing in the wretched and parsimonious conduct of the different Governments? Was the paltry pittance of sixty or seventy thousand pounds for a National Gallery, which seems to have been wrung with difficulty from the authorities, such a sum as it befitted the English nation to bestow, whilst a little kingdom in Germany expends more than three or four times the amount on a similar structure? Let the public consider these things before the profession is accused of deficiency of talent, and let it also keep in view how the patronage of this country has till lately always been confined to three architects, and there will be found sufficient apology, were the art indeed at that low ebb, to which those who are really attempting to mislead the public describe it to be sunk.

J. G.

Abingdon Street, Westminster,
March 3, 1837.

POSTSCRIPT TO PREFACE.

SINCE the above was written, the thirty-seventh number of the Foreign Quarterly Review has appeared, containing another article (on the Influence of Construction on Style in Architecture) by apparently the same reviewer, who had previously undertaken to instruct the public and the professors in the principles of architectural taste.

As usual, the titles of some German books are placed at the head of the article, which has been spun into a sort of treatise, whose object seems the recommendation to invent a totally new style of architecture, altogether founded on new expedients, and new modes of construction, by which the art is to be advanced and driven " out of its beaten track." This article exhibits little in substance that is not found in those noticed in the body of this book, except the lucubrations of Dr. Ritgen, in behalf of the banishment, for ever, of all antient styles, and founding a totally new one. This may afford considerable amusement. I should not have noticed it, but that the reviewer has most

unfeelingly raked up all the bad points of the late Sir
John Soane's private character for the purpose of holding it up to the contempt of the public.   It is not my
business to be the defender of Sir John Soane.   His
buildings, though I cannot say I admire them, were not
without merit, especially in the plans, which no architect
knew better to compose and arrange than he.   Neither
can I justify the unforgiving disposition which alienated
his property from those to whom he was bound
by natural ties ; but as respects his moral character, I
think his call to that tribunal, where he must answer
for his deeds done in the flesh, might have exempted
him and his memory from the barbarous remarks
contained in this very heavy article ; remarks utterly
irrelative to, and unconnected with the subject discussed, and hence totally foreign to the professed object
of the reviewer.   I cannot but think the Editor of this
review will regret he suffered them to escape his
pruning knife.

SECTION I.

LAWS OF PROPORTION.

THOUGH the following pages do not pretend to treat
on the principles of beauty in architecture, nor to
develope the means by which it may be attained in
architectural composition, it is necessary to consider some of the leading laws, or rather elements,
on which those principles seem to be founded. The
attempt will be made in as concise a manner as the
nature of the subject will admit. Where much appears
doubtful, it is not to be expected that what may be
advanced will be satisfactory to all; but if nothing
very disputable appear, the consideration of the question will be in some measure useful.

The science whereby the first principles* in all the
arts are derived from the effect which certain combinations have on the mind, as connected with nature and
right reason, has received the name of Æsthetics.†

* " Principles in art are no other than the trains of ideas, which arise in
" the mind of the artist out of a just and adequate consideration of all those
" local, temporary, or accidental circumstances upon which their propriety or
"impropriety—their congruity or incongruity, wholly depend."—*Payne Knight's*
Analytical Inquiry into the Principles of Taste.

† From the Greek word 'Αισθητικὸς, that is, having the power of perception
by means of the senses.

All art in its relation to nature is subject to the same
laws which affect nature itself; and if we could be
certain that the rules of art, which are the result of
reason, were necessarily connected with sensation, it
would not be difficult to frame a code of laws on which
the principles of art might be firmly founded. An illustration of what is here meant, is the rule in architecture which disallows placing over a void or opening a
mass, which appears without adequate support. Herein
an unpleasant sensation is produced in the mind, and
it appears almost possible to connect this sensation
with the rules of reason; yet in this case it seems
difficult to satisfy one's self of the exact process which
operates on the mind, without a recurrence to primitive
types, and thence pursuing the enquiry. In the other
arts, wherein the immediate type is nature herself, the
difficulty of establishing such laws is obviously lessened.
The Germans have latterly employed themselves on
the doctrine of æsthetics as applied to architecture;
among them * Wolff has very properly deduced the
principles of the art from the general laws of gravitation, and the necessity of producing equilibrium and
stability by the counteraction of weight for weight, or
a counteraction to the laws of gravitation. The theory
issound; but the celebrated and ingenious work of
Lebrun,† on which much is founded of what the following pages contain, deprives Wolff of any claim to

* Beiträge zur æsthetik der Baukunst, 1834.

† Theorie de l'Architecture Grecque et Romaine, deduite de l'Analise
des Monumens Antiques. Folio, Paris, 1807.

originality, and it is rather extraordinary that the
reviewer of the German, in a late number of the
Foreign Quarterly, appears to have been altogether
unaware of Lebrun's work, which he otherwise, one
would suppose, must have noticed. But to return to
the doctrine of æsthetics; a synopsis of it may be
shortly given as follows.

The ESSENCE of the polite arts is to be found in
expression, or the power of representation, by lines,
words, or any other media: such expression arising
from an exercise of the inventive faculty. Their END
is the production of pleasurable sensation; whereas in
the sciences the *ends* sought are instruction and
utility. In eloquence and in poetry, it is true, the
end is to instruct, as in architecture it is to attain an
useful result; yet the expression on which they depend
brings them within the scope of those laws which
govern the fine arts, whose OBJECT is beauty. BEAUTY
is the result of all the various perfections whereof a
object is susceptible, such perfections being dependent on the AGREEABLE PROPORTIONS between the
several parts of the same object, and on the proportions between each part and that object as a whole.
GENIUS, or the power of inventing, is the faculty by
which the mind is enabled to conceive and express its
conceptions; whilst TASTE, or the natural sensation
of a mind refined by art, guides genius in discerning,
embracing, and producing beauty.

It is perhaps no very bold assumption, that
the most perfect notion we conceive of stability results

from the contemplation of an horizontal line ; whilst, on the contrary, a vertical line produces a directly opposite feeling, namely, that of instability. This idea may be carried out as in the diagram, wherein the general form of a Gothic spire, and the pediment of a Grecian portico are inclosed within the pleasing form of an Egyptian pyramid. The last, which seems calculated for eternal endurance, comparatively approaches horizontality, and gives an idea of firmness and stability ; whilst the first seems to possess but a tottering equilibrium, tottering in proportion to the decrease of its base. The pediment is, however, subject to different laws, which it is not necessary to touch upon. Stability is of course dependent on the laws of gravitation, to which, under the division of Statics, a strict atten- is no less necessary in the other fine arts than in architecture. Thus it appears that at least one of the reasons to be given for the beauty of the pyramidal form arises from the stability or state of rest which it seems to possess. Rest, repose, stability, balance— perhaps, all meaning the same thing, are the essential ingredients in architectural beauty, and every building which indicates the want of these qualities, induces an unpleasant sensation : witness the celebrated Cam- panile at Pisa, and the perhaps still more extraor- dinary Asinelli and Garisendi towers at Bologna ; so of all this class, which never can be made agreeable subjects for the painter's pencil.

Where are to be sought the primitive types of

architecture ? If the question could be satisfactorily answered, the discovery would only be important as leading to the solution of those points requiring certain arrangements which limit the propriety or impropriety, the congruity or incongruity, of certain forms of detail. Thus the capital of a column seems to point to a timber type, wherein its spreading at the upper part affords a greater bearing or area of support for the beam it sustains. But the hypothesis of a hut origin is wholly inconsistent with the history of the art. Egyptian architecture points to a widely different origin, namely, that of subterraneous habitations, and the architecture of Asia equally indicates a similar origin. That elegant and most accomplished writer, Quatremere de Quincy, has spoken of the three classes of mankind to whom different sorts of dwellings were originally suitable. First, the Hunters [among whom he classes the Ichthyophagi], who, he presumes, used the caverns of the rock for their dwellings in preference to those formed by their own hands. The pastoral class, who, from the necessity of constantly changing the pasturage for their herds and flocks, led a wandering life, and dwelt in tents : and lastly, the agricultural class, who, from fixing themselves to a spot, found it necessary to build solid, fixed, and substantial habitations, as well for the protection of themselves from the elements, as for the preservation of the fruits of the earth which their industry had raised. These dwellings M. de

* Art. *Architecture*, Encyclopedie Methodique.

Quincy assumes to have been the type of what is strictly denominated architecture.* But it appears past question, that some of the columns and entablatures of Egypt had precedence, in point of antiquity, of the earliest temples of Greece; and as, if that be granted, all that was required in regard to further invention was the method of roofing buildings, which no less from their extent than the want of stone blocks must have been covered by an assemblage of timbers, it seems that without recurrence to timber construction, prototypes for Grecian architecture are to be found among the venerable remains of Egypt.†

After all that has been written on the subject, it would appear that the orders which are the distinguishing features of the works of the ancients, are the result of the experience and working of ages, founded, doubtless, upon types which, from geometrical principles of poise and counterpoise, in their nature unalterable, were very slowly perfected; and though they might have been varied, or new orders invented, the latter must have been conformable in general principles to those on which the ancient orders were first contrived. If a very strict analysis be instituted,

---

* C'est incontestablement la charpente, qui a servi de Modèle à l'Architecture Grecque; et il faut avouer que des trois modèles que la Nature peu présenter à l'Art, celui ci est sans doute le plus parfait et le plus beau de tous. And again, Quiconque y fera attention, verra sans peine qu'il renferme par sa nature toutes les parties qni peuvent contribuer à l'utilité et à la beauté, et que la plus simple cabanne de bois contient le germe des plus magnifiques palais.

† See the Author's edition of Chambers's Civil Archit. Vol. I. page 38, where a specimen, kindly communicated by Mr. Barry, is given.

it seems doubtful whether there be more than one order, *
as a genus, whereof there are five, or, as some say, only
three species. In each, the leading or rather bounding
forms of the general mass have a great resemblance,
rising in slenderness as the order recedes from the
original type; for it seems not only universally allowed,
but certain, that the Doric order has a prior claim
in respect of antiquity to all the others.

The orders have been the principal basis for all
the manipulations (as they may be called) in architectural composition; and as readiness in applying
them seems to have always been one of the first
objects at which young architects have aimed—so
much so that they scarcely seem to consider a design
worthy the epithet architectural without the display
of a portico, or at least some half dozen columns
attached to a wall, to which they are generally more
an incumbrance than an ornament—the facility of
their application has often superseded all considera-
tions of propriety. This, in some measure, has
arisen from placing more reliance on pictorial effect
than propriety. That readiness of hand and effect,
as respects pictorial composition in architecture, is
very frequently attained without a thorough acquaintance on the part of the architect with the fundamental
principles of the art he professes, is well known. It is
with those who possess those qualifications, an affair
of the eye and the hand, unguided by judgment,

* Lebrun's definition of an order is, "a combination of support and load,
duly adjusted to the effect contemplated by the artist." It is rather general.

but mostly founded upon observation * of works which
have been accounted beautiful by the common consent
of mankind : in truth, such have " no reason for the
faith that is in them." With others, who exhibit less
genius, the adaptation of the models of antiquity,
piled piecemeal on each other, as we see in the present
German school, interlarded with morsels of a later
period, sometimes succeeds; but the success is altogether
a matter of chance. In either case the result is most
probably defect or excess in material. Again, public
institutions and academies vastly increase candidates
for fame, though the quantity of genius and talent
remains the same ; and under such disadvantages is it
extraordinary, among crowds of competitors who
are every hour rising, that many would never have
become such, but for the encouragement of patrons,
whereby the voice of those few whom nature and
education has gifted with the requisite judgment is
lost in the silly, noisy, and forward opinions of shallow
smatterers in art ?

But I wander from the subject, and it is now
time to turn to one of the more immediate objects of
these pages, namely, the introduction to the reader
of the theory laid down by Lebrun. This was first
noticed in my edition of Chambers's Civil Architecture, in 1825, but seems nevertheless to have attracted

---

* Observation alone, without principles, will never make more than an
ordinary artist. Authorities are only good when the principles that formed them
are reverted to—without that, they make the artist a machine, instead of an
intellectual being.

so little attention in this country, as to be scarcely seen in a catalogue of books, though on the continent it has met with a very different reception. If it can be shewn that those buildings of antiquity * which are universally accounted beautiful, exhibit a certain constancy in their proportions of weight and loading, it seems but a fair inference that their beauty, must, at least in a great degree, if not altogether, be the result of those proportions. Perhaps, if the subject were pursued *au fond*, it would be found that on these proportions might depend not only the requisites of magnitude and strength, which in construction are the qualities which affect the eye—those of order and harmony, which in design are qualities affecting the understanding, but even the requisites of richness and simplicity, which are qualities more especially exciting the affections. Moreover, the principles in question will be found to involve the science of construction, which, to the architect, is what execution is to the painter, without which respectively neither can embody his ideas.

* If the subject were pursued in respect of the pointed architecture of Europe, there is no doubt a very similar constancy of proportion would be found. My other occupations at this moment have not allowed me time for much investigation on the subject; but I find that in Salisbury Cathedral, a section through the buttresses gives the proportion of voids to solids as 34 to 25 nearly—in King's College Chapel it approaches equality. This subject is well worthy of further investigation : it has never yet been taken up, and in the hands of a competent person would doubtless lead to some very curious results. The thrusts in Gothic vaulting are actually less (being inversely as the sines of the angles) than in buildings covered with semi-circular arches, hence a diminution in the thickness of the piers. Equipoise in these is equivalent to the abstract stability which is the subject discussed.

Lebrun's division of architecture is into two parts, one whereof he denominates " Architecture of Stability," the other, "Decorative Architecture." The former is that in which the columns actually support the superincumbent parts; the other, that in which they are only accessories: but the application of his theory will be found the same in each, though the assertion of Galiani does not quite bear out the latter hypothesis.*

In the subjoined diagrams, I. and II. are what Lebrun calls the radical types of flat and circular arches. No. I. needs little demonstra- 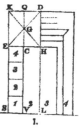 tion. It will be directly seen, that G is the centre of gravity of the half loading, or burthen KEDH, which is equal to the half opening CHVL, and also equal to the support ECSV. On the right hand side of the figure is shewn the mode of subdividing the load, for the introduc- tion of architectural details. In diagram 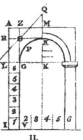 II. the burthen will be found equal, or nearly so, to the support, though at the first glance it is not so obvious. The two surfaces, ALGZ, and ZGMN, may not be exactly equal, for the triangle GON is incommensurable ; but, dispensing with strict mathematical precision, we may take the surface of the circle inscribed in the square, equal to three quarters

* Qual che non può sussistere veramente e realmente, non può ne anco esser, approvato, ancorchè fatto in apparenza. — *Galiani in Vitruv.*

of the square.   The triangle GON, and the rectangle
RAZO, will be a sixteenth part of the square; or,
which is the same thing, equal the square of half the
radius.   Hence the two parts of the burthen, ROLG
and MZON, will be equal.   In respect of the supports,
one half only of the burthen acts on the support,
because of the distance of its centre of gravity from
the vertical ZG.   But this centre is somewhere in a
supposed line, PA, directed towards the centre of the
arch, since APLG is equal to APMN.   Thus the
common centre of the two parallelograms, AMRN
and AZLG, is in O, in the direction QC.   Hence, by
adding the incommensurable triangle ONG, the centre
of gravity will be somewhere from P to O ; and since
the weight overhanging, and that whose bearing is
solid, are equal, ZGMN, which overhangs, draws, or
thrusts AZLG, on account of the distance of the centre
of gravity in OP, from the vertical ZG ; for were the
direction of the centre in the vertical, the action either
way would be annihilated.   This being so, divide the
surface of half the arcade by the width LG, and the
rectangle LGIV is obtained.   From this equality of
the burthen and support, the height of the arch is
found to be equal to twice its width.   The right hand
side of the diagram, as in that preceding, is filled up
architecturally.   In the above examples, which are of
pleasing proportions, it will be seen that the voids are
equal to the superincumbent masses, and that the
supports are equal to the burthens imposed.

Although the limits prescribed to these pages will

not permit the full developement of M. Lebrun's theory, it must be examined a little further; for whether it were known to the Greeks or not, there is so wonderful a coincidence between *its* principles and *their* practice, that the reader must be struck with the comparison. Michael Angelo said his compasses were in his eye; and if what is conjectured be unfounded, truly indeed may the same be said of the architects of antiquity.

In the subjoined diagram we have the type of an Hexastyle temple. Its width is twice the height of the columns, which being six diameters high, the extent of the whole front becomes 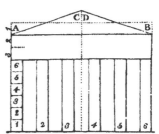 equal to 12 diameters. If, from these 12 diameters, we subtract the six which the columns themselves occupy, the five voids or intercolumniations are equal to six diameters. The loading or burthen will be as follows:—The height of the entablature, without the pediment, is two diameters, and as its half length is the height of a column, so each half is equal to two columns, or the whole is equal to four. The whole pediment being two diameters high, and the triangles, A and B, being equal to the triangles C and D above the dotted line, it follows that is equal to two columns, which, added to the four in the entablature, make in the whole six, which are equal to the five voids, and also equal to the six supports.

Science, such as is seen in the edifices of the pointed

style, wherein the thrusts of their stone vaultings are balanced by buttresses and the like, must be introduced when the simple principle of weight for weight is not the guide. *   It must not be supposed by the student, that having possessed himself of such a doctrine as is here presented, which is infinite in the variety it is capable of producing, both in columns and their intercolumniations, there are no other points in designing requisite for the creation of beauty, and to which his most unwearied attention is necessary.

Decoration and proper disposition of the details, so that they be in harmony with the general character and leading forms of the edifice, require that genius and intelligence which always distinguish the great from the mediocre artist.   One of the canons of a reviewer, who will be often quoted in the following pages, and which may as well be noted here as here-

* In five celebrated examples, taken for the purpose of ascertaining whether there be any accordance between the theory and ancient practice, the subjoined results exhibit a singular confirmation of some such theory as is spoken of in this place. The superficies of the columns, cut through their axes vertically by a plane parallel to the front of the building, are compared with the area of the entablature of each respectively. The weights of each being as the cubes of the square roots of the areas, will equally represent the supports and weights in either of the terms.

In the *Parthenon*, the supports are to the weights, as   1546 : 1843, or 1 : 1.19
If the steps be reckoned, then as ....2183 : 1843, or 1 : 0.84
In the *Doric Portico*, the supports are to the weights, as 4070 : 3990, or 1 : 0.98
In the *Pseudo dipteral Temple at Pæstum*, the supports
  are to the weights, as .... 1090 : 1103, or 1 : 1.01
In the *Temple of Erectheus*, the supports are to the
  weights, as .... 2640 : 2800, or 1 : 1.07
In the *Pantheon at Rome*, the supports are to the
  weights, as .... 1566 : 1723, or 1 : 1.10
—*Note, Page* 160, *to my Edition of Chambers's Civil Architecture.*

after, is, " that the Doric seems to require FLAT SCULP-
TURE, while the Ionic may be allowed that which is
stronger, yet not so bold as what should be reserved
for the Corinthian. Some," he says, " may consider
this classification not only fantastic, but incongruous ;
inasmuch as we here assign the boldest style of relief
to the most delicate of the orders, and the most delicate
of that species of sculpture to the boldest of them." *
Certainly to me it appears not only fantastical, but
little short of nonsensical, and a mere dictum of the
reviewer, without recurrence to the very first principles of design. Notwithstanding the great contempt for ancient authorities, which it is the fashion
in the present day for writers to exhibit, it is impossible to avoid putting the reviewer's canon of art in
juxta-position with the extraordinary sculptures of
extremely high and bold relief, which decorated the
metopæ of the Parthenon, after which no comment can
be necessary—that is, if the reader, like myself, be of
opinion, that the temple in question is one possessing consummate beauty.

But to return to the further consideration of Lebrun's work. It has been already observed, that in
Decorative Architecture, the columns employed are
merely accessories to the stability of the building.
Yet this species of architecture has its foundation on
the same principles as that in which the columns really
carry the superincumbent entablature. Its variety, in
respect of proportions, is as infinite as in the last

* Foreign Quarterly, No. XXVII. p. 101.

example. The subjoined diagram,
which will briefly explain how this
arises, is a combination of the
species, in which the columns are ten
diameters high, and are applied to
piers equal in surface to the voids.
In the example, the superficies of entablature is equal
to the columns. The height of the arcade is equal to
double its width, and the impost is equal to the architrave. This, as well as the examples preceding,
so closely resemble one which would be produced by
adherence to the rules prescribed for arcades in almost
all architectural works of the best authors, that one is
surprised, as I have before observed, at the remarkable
coincidence between the principles of Lebrun, and the
actual practice of the earliest architects.

The reviewer before referred to says he has looked
at the principles of the ancients, " after the same
fashion that a mere grammarian reads the Greek
poets; the spirit of their works is with him a very
secondary consideration ; what he chiefly perceives in
them, is articles and aorists, peculiarities of construction and dialects, longs and shorts. In like manner,
architects attach too much importance to diameters,
modules, and minutes." *   No doubt, the longs and
shorts, which have met with loud and deep curses
from most schoolboys, and perhaps from the reviewer
himself when *in statu pupillari*, are restraints imposed

* Foreign Quarterly, No. XXVII.

upon versification; they have been submitted to
for ages, and are likely still so to be. Habits
of attention are, nevertheless, engendered by them,
and they have not unfrequently produced a happy
method of expressing a thought. Not less has
a strict adherence to the laws of symmetry and proportion been frequently serviceable to the architect in
creating, or rather suggesting expedients, which have
given the highest value to his design. The fact is,
notwithstanding the *dictum* of the reviewer, that the
æsthetic value of all works of art, and most especially
those which are architectural, is dependent on the
"elementary and technical" rules and studies to which
he says too much importance is attached. "So greatly
do the varieties of the same order differ from each
other, that, assuming, as some have done, proportion
to be the chief distinction between one order and another, and that each admits of only certain specific
proportions, we must subdivide each class into several
subordinate ones."* This is but a superficial view of
the case, as the reader will find by reference to the
note at page 13, wherein the relation of weights and
supports to each other is given from several celebrated
buildings. Two examples, than which in appearance it
is impossible to produce specimens of greater apparent
dissimilarity, will shew how the ancients were guided by
certain laws, which, notwithstanding the restraint
which the reviewer wants to shake off, admit of a

* Foreign Quarterly Review, No. XXVII.

variety which, on comparing them, will be obvious to
the least educated.   These are the orders (both
Doric) used in the Hypæthral Temple at Pæstum, and
the Portico of Philip.   In the former the columns are
only $4\frac{134}{1000}$ diameters high, in the latter $6\frac{535}{1000}$ diameters,
and yet the heights of their whole entablatures
in terms of their diameters, vary only $\frac{12}{100}$ of that
diameter, that of the former being 1·74, of the latter,
1·86.   Now here at once is opened, through the laws
of architecture, a field for varying the proportions of
the columns themselves, which all ages can never
exhaust; and yet, says the reviewer, "supposing the
attention bestowed by us upon Greek architecture to
have been to any purpose at all, we must surely have
been convinced, ere this, that the doctrine so long
maintained, in regard to proportions, *ought to be dis-
carded as untenable*, or at least, required to be amended
and remodelled."   The reviewer has here exhibited so
slender a knowledge of the philosophy of the art, that
the further notice which will be hereafter taken of his
criticisms may, to many, seem unnecessary and un-
called for.   But the present method of reviewing
works of art, and the assumed importance of a certain
set of writers on architecture, render it expedient to
give the reader some notion of the justice with which
they put themselves forward as connoisseurs, and
whether they are not *conoscitori senza cognizione.*

In the disposition of orders above orders, the upper
order will always want that exact stability which the prin-

ciples require.   The lower order being ar-
ranged as in the diagram, it will be seen, on
inspection, that the centre of gravity G, is in
the prolongation of a vertical line from the
inner sides of the columns; but in the upper
row of columns, the centre of gravity G, of
the loading, will necessarily fall nearer the
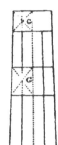
central line, for the lower diameter of the upper columns
cannot be larger than the upper diameter of the lower
ones.   Hence, in architecture of two orders, if the
columns be insulated, the upper order must, in some
measure, be deficient in the stability which the theory
requires.

Such, then, are the leading principles on which
Lebrun has contended that the ancients conducted
their designs; and it has been more than once observed
in the preceding pages, that there is every rational
appearance of their truth, from their being so borne
out by the test of early examples.   The student, if he
would pursue the matter further, has the means of
doing it from the few examples given; but a reference
to the author would be, of course, more valuable to
him.   The architect is as much bound by rules, which
cannot be violated without diverging from the path of
correct taste, as the author is by the sound rules of
criticism; and there can be no reason for such devia-
tion by either, since the new combinations, which may
be still found under the system which has endured for
ages, are as many and infinite as may be derived in

musical composition from the different sounds of the musical scale.   Let not, then, the student suppose that novelty and originality subject him to the restraint of which so much has been said in this section, or that the multitudinous changes, which are always within the reach of his art, CAN EVER be exhausted. They are infinite.

SECTION II.

GRECIAN ARCHITECTURE.

THE term GRECIAN Architecture is so frequently misused, that it will be well to premise, here, my intention to confine its use rigorously to those buildings whose parts are so strictly derived from Grecian examples, that even the contours of the mouldings employed are confined to portions of Conic Sections.   It is a constant, but very improper practice, and tending very much to mislead the public, to call a building Grecian, merely because its composition embraces one of the three orders, which, originally invented by the Greeks, were much changed, both in detail and proportions, in after ages by the Romans.   It will be easily perceived, therefore, that the introduction of the arch and dome into Grecian composition, is totally irreconcileable with the notions I entertain of architectural propriety.   The opinions of M. Klenze and

c 2

the Foreign Quarterly Reviewer, * do not at all shake
my opinion, however beautiful and simple they, as
well even as I, may consider its form. It can scarcely
be necessary, in this place, to remind the reader, that
till after the reign of Alexander every circumstance is
against the probability of the use of arches, constructed on scientific principles. †   During the reign
of Alexander a great change took place in the arts
and sciences of Greece, and improvement was effected
far beyond what former ages had witnessed.   It is not
unlikely that the arch was invented by the Greeks,
and the use of it by them taught to the Romans. This,
however, is matter of conjecture.   The reviewer himself allows that‡ "mouldings ought to conform with the
character of the order; and, besides, great reserve
and discretion in *introducing them at all*, arches
should be made to seem to blend naturally with the
rest of the composition." Before such blending is ever
accomplished, the nature of pure Greek architecture
must be changed.   The columnar style, as used by
the Greeks, rendered the arch unnecessary; hence its
introduction will always appear, to the educated eye,
inharmonious, inappropriate, and incapable of amal-
gamation with the solemn majesty and purity of Greek
composition.   To me it has always appeared much
the same thing, and quite as incongruous a combina-

* No. XXVII. page 108.

† Rumours and statements of the discovery of the arch recently made by travellers in Egypt, are not sufficiently satisfactory to my mind, without very correct drawings of construction and authentic dates of erection.

‡ No. XXVII. page 109.

tion, as spanning the interval between two Corinthian columns with a pointed arch, whereof examples exist.

The chief remains of Grecian architecture consist of religious edifices; and there is much truth in an observation made in a periodical published many years ago, "that it requires no common skill to apply it to those of a different destination, without either violating its character, or conveying to the building the air of an heathen temple. The Italian style, whose origin is dated from the revival of the arts, although popularly denominated Grecian, and although founded upon the Greek and Roman orders, has nevertheless necessarily acquired a character distinct from that of the preceding: less severe in its form, less chaste in its decorations—it is more pliant, more varied, more picturesque." The Greeks threw all their force into the splendour and magnificence of their temples, and, though at a late period,* their private dwellings began to exhibit appearances of luxury, but little attention was till then bestowed on their private houses. In, or rather to, them it is very difficult to conceive any application of their orders, except in open courts, similar to the *atrium* of the Romans. Vitruvius, whose authority is surely valuable in matters of fact whereof he was witness, though it is very much the fashion in these days to treat him with unmeasured contempt, tells us, † that in his days the ruins of the building, wherein the Areopagus assembled, were still

* Demosthenes, Orat adv. Aristocratem.
† Lib. II. cap. I.

visible, and that this was but a very miserable sort of structure. To return to the private dwelling : it is certain that it frequently, in some parts, consisted of more than one story, * notwithstanding some learned men have doubted that fact. Further than these points all is now conjecture. It must not, however, be forgotten, that, besides sacred edifices, we are not entirely without other examples, such as Propylea, in which columns are very principal features, and those columns in every respect similar to such as are used in the Temple. Again, we have the Choragic monuments, exquisite specimens of the art, in one of which, namely, that of Lysicrates, no grace nor refinement of the art is wanting.

In Grecian architecture we find little variety of invention ; but in what was done, selection of form, fine combination, and great unity in arrangement and use of detail, are universally prevalent. It has in almost every treatise been stated, that there is a difference found in the proportions of its orders among each other ; but from what has been shown in Sect. I., it must be granted that such does not exist, and that the thickness or slenderness of a column does not affect the general proportions of the order itself, as respects the principles on which the whole combination is founded.

When architecture has arrived at such a stage of perfection that it is sanctioned by the approval of ages, any important change in it is scarcely admissible,

---

* Iliad, B. 514. 16, 184.

neither is it easily effected; all the advice, therefore, to the artist, which is found in recent writings, to emancipate himself from the trammels under which he is said to be labouring, is absurd.   What the critics require of him is to carry on, if it may be so termed, the principles of Greek art, as found in sacred build-ings, into modern edifices and dwellings, which is much the same thing as to require a man to invent a language, equally suited to the ordinary inter-course of all classes of society, and the lofty flights of the poet.   The truth is, that the arrangements which Greek architecture require, in order to produce effect, are unsuitable to modern habits.   If it be intended merely to urge the architect to enter into the feelings that actuated the mind of the ancient artist, it is granted immediately that such is his proper course ; but this will involve no more than general principles, namely, those which point to the leading requisites in a design dependent on form, unity, combination, and stability.   And will any one allege that this has not been done repeatedly since the extinction of archi-tecture in Greece.—Had Rome really nothing to boast ?—Are the extraordinary Gothic edifices of the continent of Europe, and no less of this country, un-profitable specimens of design and execution ?—Shall condemnation to infamy pass on the splendid palaces of Italy, and the whole of the buildings of France and this country ? England, however, must be mentioned with an apology, for the reviewer* states, that here

* No. XXXV. page 160.

the professors " afford proof how imperfectly every
style of architecture appears to be understood, what
exclusive and limited views are taken of it, and how
very far our architects are from possessing sound and
well based theoretical principles, independent of con-
ventional and accidental forms, and applicable to their
art in the abstract." Without stopping to enquire
what this writer means by *accidental forms applicable
to the art in the abstract,* may it not be asked, whether
this sentence passed upon a whole profession by an
amateur, who from his writing is but slenderly versed
in the art, is not written with an acerbity which shows
some latent feeling arising from want of homage to
amateurs on the part of the professors. It would be
refreshing to see one of the designs of any of the
amateurs and critics, who, like the reviewer, pronounce
judgment on a body of men whose lives are passed
in the study of the art.

     I think it far from useless to enquire to what de-
gree of success have been carried all the attempts in
this country, and on the continent, to adapt the architecture of the Greeks to modern edifices. I am not
aware of a single felicitous attempt. Yet, with the
exception, perhaps, of the Foreign Quarterly Reviewer, it will not be asserted, by any one, that all the
artists who have tried the experiment have been men
devoid of talent. It would be easy to produce abund-
ance of examples, many of them in the metropolis ; but
the object of these pages is not to criticise the works
of my cotemporaries. On the other hand, how many

buildings have risen up during the last few years, wherein the architects, emancipating themselves from the fashion of the day, have produced works not only creditable to England, but very far superior to any other modern architecture, that of France only excepted. In truth, the day-spring is again opening upon us in this country.

As much alive to, and susceptible of, the perfection of Grecian architecture to the extent it was carried, as any of its most ardent admirers, I, many years ago, * ventured, and dangerous ground it was then to tread, upon an expression of my sentiments in this respect, and I have had the satisfaction of seeing, in all the buildings of any importance that have since been erected (I do not harbour the vanity of supposing it was the effect of " my thunder"), a gradual return to the principles of that school which, from the time of Inigo Jones to Lord Burlington, gave to the English rank among the nations of Europe, and entitled them to that homage which they have received at the hands of foreigners. † To their disgrace be it recorded, the only slanderers of English artists are among their own countrymen.

The public will, perhaps, be informed by reviewers, that new lights have broken in upon us by the discovery, or rather greater knowledge, of the produc-

* Preface to my edition of Chambers' Civil Arch.

† Speaking of Lord Burlington, Milizia says, " Si e contraddistinto tra' signori Inglesi per il suo fino gusto nelle belle arti, e spezialmente nell' Architettura." The new School of the Reviewer would give a different account of this nobleman's taste.

tions of art in Greece; but it must be recollected, that
though those works have been at the service of the
architect through the valuable labours of Stuart, the
Dilettanti Society and others, now (from the beginning)
three quarters of a century, the use and application of
Greek orders and profiles seems to be decreasing in
the inverse ratio of the time passed over, and Italian
architecture is fast regaining its original sway, and
the hold it occupied a century since in the minds of
professors.   Great, however, as is my veneration for
the antiquities of Greece, and the purity and excellence of its architecture, the study whereof I would
ever strongly recommend to the young architect as a
guide to the attainment of much that is indispensable
to make him superior to the mere builder, I must
declare, that, compared with the extraordinary structures of the pointed style that are scattered over
Europe, the most celebrated works of the Greeks sink
into nothingness.   Unity and harmony, symmetry and
beauty of proportion, are not less discernible in the
edifices of the middle ages than in the most celebrated
temples of the Greeks; but beyond these qualifications, the first exhibit almost fearful examples of
counterpoise and technical skill, united with a dura-
bility and stability which at the first glance seem to
belong exclusively to the last.   It is, however, difficult
to institute a comparison between any two differing
styles of architecture: I must nevertheless not omit to
glance at the cathedrals of Cologne and Strasbourg,
but more particularly the choir, the only finished

part, of the former; and small on plan as it is, compared with some of the tremendous remnants of antiquity, what an overpowering effect is produced by it! With what extreme apparent facility the prodigious thrusts of the vaulting are resisted, and a counterpoise obtained by means which externally are converted into the greatest beauties, a system whereof the Greeks had no conception. Their architects piled stones on stones; but the architects of the middle ages reared vaulting in the air. It has before been hinted, that the latter seem to have had some general relative principles of stability, not very dissimilar to those which form the subject of section I.; certainty, as in the other case, there is none, and it is greatly to be deplored that in both cases all rules are lost. The architects, or rather freemasons, of the middle ages, have left us no precepts; but whatever might have been the principles on which they proceeded in their surprising structures, they were distinguished by the most profound and scientific knowledge of architecture—an art then in such great requisition, that the number of examples they have left us is quite astonishing. To use a mercantile phrase, could the demand be again created, there would soon appear both in this country and elsewhere a supply of artists capable of producing similar works; but till that time arrives, all the endeavours in any country to reintroduce pointed architecture will be vain. The whole nation must require it. The love for its employment in the dwellings of a few noblemen and gentlemen in

the country, is a drop of water in the ocean : nor will
the encouragement with which it has met by its use in
a single large public building, in which its leading
features of poise and counterpoise cannot be introduced,
and in others would be absurd, ever restore its general
application.   The reader must pardon this digression
into pointed architecture.   On a favourite subject it
is difficult to be silent, but the observations may not be
unserviceable.   What object is gained by the adoption
of Gothic or Elizabethan architecture, as it is called?
Does it afford an opportunity of disposing a plan more
commodiously than Grecian, or Roman, or Italian
architecture? Are either more strictly national styles?
Certainly no.   The former is beyond question of German origin, as the latter is of Italian, and that tran-
sition style which floated between Gothic and classical
architecture.   True, it is picturesque ; but so also is the
architecture of the Florentine school.   The legislature
has nevertheless determined that they will try the
experiment; and notwithstanding all the talent of the
artist on whom the choice has fallen, it will not
satisfy,—whilst the same artist, employed on a building in the Italian style, would, I have no doubt, produce
an edifice worthy of himself and the country, and at
much less cost.

Some have thought that the temples at Pæstum exhibit more severe simplicity and perfection
of design than the edifices of Athens, and that the
former are in a more correct and classical style.   Dr.
Clarke* says that Lusieri was of this opinion, and

* Travels in Greece.

that he considered, that "in those buildings the Doric
order attained a pre-eminence beyond which it never
passed; not a stone has been placed there without some
evident and important design; every part of the structure bespeaks its own essential utility." He thought
similarly of the temple of Jupiter in the island of
Ægina. "Of such a nature," adds Lusieri, "were
works in architecture, when the whole aim of the
architect was to unite grandeur with utility; the former
being founded on the latter. All then was truth,
strength, and sublimity." One of the reasons for this
preference is curious enough, and will almost excite a
smile; it is, that there are "defects, arising from
improper conduct at the Parthenon on the part of the
builders; * and he specifies as one, the vacuities above
the architrave behind the metopæ and triglyphs sufficiently spacious for a person to walk in, whereas at
Pæstum the same parts of the works are solid stone."

One of the beauties tending to give effect to the
edifices of Greece, has been, on the testimony of almost all travellers, the colour of the materials whereof
they are composed. Dr. Clarke observes that a warm
ochreous tint is diffused over all the buildings of the
Acropolis, which *he* says is peculiar to the ruins of
Athens. "Perhaps to this warm colour, so remark-
ably characterising the remains of ancient buildings at
Athens, Plutarch alluded in that beautiful passage
cited by Chandler,† where *he affirmed that the struc-*

* Clarke's Travels in Greece.
† In Vitâ Pericl.

*tures of Pericles possessed a peculiar and unparalleled
excellence of character ; a certain freshness bloomed
upon them, and preserved their faces uninjured, as if
they possessed a never-fading spirit, and had a soul
insensible to age.*"* It is odd enough that recent
discoveries incontestably prove this species of beauty
not to have existed originally, for it is now pretty well
ascertained that it was the practice of the Greeks to
paint the whole of the inside and outside of their
temples in party colours. It was previously well
known that it was one of their practices to paint ornaments on particular parts of a building ; but M. Schau-
bert, the architect of the king of Greece, has found
that this was by no means the extent to which painting was carried,† and M. Semper, another German
architect, has completely corroborated the fact in his
examination of the temple of Theseus. It is by no
means impossible nor uncommon for a person to be
alive to beauty of form without having a proper perception or feeling of the beauty resulting from
harmony in colouring; hence it is not to be assumed,
because the Greeks were addicted to the practice
above mentioned, that their taste in other respects is
not worthy of all the admiration that it has received.
Egypt was doubtless the country whence this custom
was imported, and though it is difficult to judge of the

* It is curious that the last traveller, the Rev. Christopher Words-
worth, should have also considered the colour of the ruins one of the ingredients of their beauty. "Athens and Attica."

† A. F. Von Quast—Mittheilungen über Alt and Neu Athen.

effect produced by the gaudy colouring of buildings, without seeing a specimen, I confess I am disinclined to believe it possible to have had any other than a wretched and barbarous effect. The last building of any magnitude which has seen risen in this metropolis, is the National Gallery—one in which there is neither unity, harmony, symmetry, nor simplicity ; and inasmuch as it is, architecturally speaking,

———-——nullâ virtute redemptum
A vitiis,

and as no tricks that could be played with it could do it any harm, I think it might be no bad scheme, to paint it in brilliant party colours for the purpose of trying the experiment, and thus setting the question at rest. Before quitting my short notice of this singular specimen of architecture, I cannot help expressing my opinion, that the public are infinitely indebted to the little coterie that got up this job, inasmuch as it is more than unlikely such another will be attempted or permitted. The sketch in the Italian style which Mr. Barry made for a façade to this building, would have been highly creditable to the nation had it met with adoption.*

The Grecian style, in its earliest works, might, perhaps, be very properly called the heroic style in architecture. Formed at a period when the science of construction was in its infancy, though the mode of raising and moving enormous blocks of stone was thoroughly understood, economy in the use of mate-

---

* The Royal Academy have just elected the architect of the wretched pile of building above alluded to, their professor of architecture !!!

rials could never have been with the Greeks a subject
of consideration, and the effect produced by their edifices
is always at the maximum of expense.   With them all
was excess, as far as the necessity for loading and counterpoise were concerned, from their not carrying out to
a greater extent the principles disclosed in the preceding
section.   The difference is quite extraordinary between
the large masses of material employed by the ancients,
and the slender pieces of stone whereof some of the
spires of the middle ages are constructed : hence,
economy and production of effect by amazingly small
comparative means.

The artist labours in vain, if there be not on the
part of the public by whom he is employed some cor-
respondent feeling, some perception of the language in
which he addresses it.   The Greeks seem to have
had, generally, such an acute feeling for art as to
have cheered their artists in the prosecution of their
studies ; there was a correspondence of understanding
between them, necessary, it is to be observed, in all
the arts, but clearly more in architecture than in the
rest, because that is not an imitative art; and, hence no
type being universally known with which it can be
compared, there exists a far greater difficulty in the
appreciation of the labours of the architect which are
his greatest encouragement, than in those arts wherein
immediate reference may be made to a type.

There is, certainly, a striking analogy between
language and architecture, not only as respects their
intelligibility by those to whom they are addressed,
but in many other points of view which were ably

pointed out some years since in a periodical, * by an *anonymous author*, to whom I am under obligation for some valuable hints, and in whose words I shall conclude this section. " There is," says the writer, " if the expression will not incur the censure of being extravagantly affected, *dead* architecture as well as *dead* language. Egypt will furnish us with an instance. In the architectural remains of that nation we may plainly discern an aboriginal style, whose characteristics are, a rude grandeur and barbarous majesty.— Often stupendous, hardly ever beautiful, vast, solemn, and displaying but little variety in its outlines; it rather seizes upon the imagination by its mysterious antiquity, and its astonishing masses, than captivates the eye by the graceful forms of its details, or the pleasing air of its fabrics. How such a style might have been modified by degrees, so as to adapt it to domestic purposes ; how its vocabulary might have been gradually extended and enriched, so as to attain all the varieties of expression of which a well digested system is capable ; how, by an uninterrupted succession of improvements, its maturity might have been effected, it would, at present, be hazardous to conjecture ; yet, confined as its powers now are, it seems able to exhibit only colossal, yet uncouth grandeur, and sepulchral gloom. These observations," says the writer, " are in a certain degree applicable to that which can alone in strictness pretend to the title of Grecian Architecture."

* Annals of the Fine Arts.

D

SECTION III.

ITALIAN SCHOOL OF ARCHITECTURE.

The very extraordinary volume published by Aldus, in 1499, which was written by a member of the Colonna Family, under the title of " *Hypneroto-machia Poliphili* " (Poliphilus' dream of the battle of love), seems to have been one of the principal incentives to, or rather incidents that quickened, the revival of architecture in Italy.   The author of it describes and groups, with great beauty and effect, the most splendid assemblages of objects of art.   Decorated with wood engravings of singular beauty, in which the details and accessaries are strictly classical, written with great spirit and elegance, its effect at the period must have been magical, and doubtless, with the aid of the celebrated treatise on architecture, by Leo. Bat. Alberti, whose appearance was nearly contemporaneous with it, little more than those two works could have been wanting to enlist all Italy, the hot-bed of art, in its restoration.   From Vasari may be gathered the distaste *for Gothic Architecture which had fully ripened when he wrote.*   Speaking of buildings in that style, he says, " Hanno più il modo da parer fatti di carta, che di pietre, o di marmo;" to which, a little

after, he ludicrously adds—" E spesso con mettere
cosa sopra cosa andavano in tanta altezza, che la fine
d'un porta toccava il tetto."

The Italian school, which finally settled itself in
the adaptation of the antient Roman orders and their
details to comparatively modern habits, was engrafted
at first on Gothic designs.   Instances of this may
be produced in the splendid loggia of Orgagna,
in Sta. M. dei Fiori, and many other buildings in
Florence, in Pisa, Siena, and other cities.   Brunelleschi seems to have emancipated himself from the
mixture of two such discordant styles.   Still there continued, as we see in the Ricardi, Strozzi, and other
palaces in Florence, a lingering love for the mixture,
of which the architects could scarcely divest themselves.
Yet, when they came to the cornices, the massive,
unbroken cornices of their palaces, the littleness of
the other parts is so completely lost, that it is evident
they were actuated by the same feelings of unity and
breadth that lent so much value to the best works of
the antients.   From the time of Brunelleschi to the
time of Borromini, with whom the Italian school
closes, indeed from the spirit of innovation and
wretched taste of this last artist, architecture seems to
have previously seen its best days, included a period
of about two hundred and seventy years, during which
so much was done, that Italy may be fairly said to
have overbuilt herself.   The total decay of that commerce, which in her palmy days she possessed, has
withdrawn, long since, the demand for new churches

and palaces, and nothing but independence can re-
store her, if even that can do it, to a high rank in art.
The period above mentioned includes the names of
Brunelleschi, Michelozzo, L. B. Alberti, Cronaca,
Bramante, Baldassare Peruzzi, Raphael Sanzio, San
Micheli, San Gallo, Julio Romano, Michel Angelo da
Buonarotti, Sansovino, Alessi, Ligorio, Vignola, Am-
manati, Palladio, Fontana, Scamozzi, Carlo Mader-
no, Bernini, and Borromini.   Among the works of
these extraordinary artists let a few be mentioned :—
The dome of Sta. Maria at Florence, for instance, by
Brunelleschi; the Palazzo della Cancellaria at Rome,
and the circular temple of S. Pietro in Montorio, by
Bramante ; the exquisite Palazzo Pandolfini, by
Raphael ; the works of San Micheli at Verona ; the
Palazzo Farnese at Rome, by San Gallo ; the cupola
of St. Peter's, raised by Michael Angelo ; the palace
of Caprarola, by Vignola ; the bridge of the Holy
Trinity at Florence by Ammanati ; the church of
the Redeemer at Venice, by Palladio ; the Procurazie
nuove in the same city, by Scamozzi : and enough
would be said, if their names were insufficient, to
prove that a never-ceasing celebrity is a never-
ending test of the genius of an artist. "Nest ce
pas," says M. Quatremere de Quincy "sur la foi
d'une semblable tradition de suffrages, que nous as-
signons encore les premiers rangs dans les arts de
la Grèce, à tant d'hommes dont toutefois les ouvrages
nous sont inconnus ?"—With such an enumeration of
the finest works of art as the reader has just seen,

will it be credited that a reviewer* has lately predicted
with great solemnity, that after a visit to " Athens
and Agrigentum, Pæstum and Pompeii," as he puts
them, with all the beauties of alliteration, the student
in architecture will finish his professional studies hereafter on the Glyptothek and Pinacothek of Klenze at
Munich, and the Wachtgebäude and Museum at Berlin.
An opportunity will afterwards occur of offering some
observations on these buildings ; in this place, the
object is merely to submit to the reader's consideration
how little such a reviewer is competent to give any
judgment of value on the Italian school of architecture, or, as far as can be gathered from his writing, on
any other school or work of art whatever.   Fielding
has said, " that the world have paid too great a com-
pliment to critics, and have imagined them men of
much greater profundity than they really are.   From
this complaisance, the critics have been emboldened to
assume a dictatorial power, and have so far succeeded,
that they are now become the masters, and have the
assurance to give laws to those authors, from whose
predecessors they originally received them."   The critic
above mentioned is not, however, yet so far advanced
in his profession as to succeed in Fielding's conclusion ;
it will require far greater powers and knowledge of
the subject than his (if it were possible) to bring
Italian architecture into discredit," or " to call in
question the talents of a Michael Angelo, a Palladio,

* Foreign Quarterly Review, No. xxvii.

or a Bernini,"* even with the anomalies that are found
in a few of their works.   Is it to follow, that because
Michael Angelo and others have been guilty of examples of false taste, that therefore they were not
great architects?   The truth is, that the Italian school
has been and still is the foundation upon which all the
buildings of Europe are designed, nor is it possible
that that system can be changed so long as the present
habits of its inhabitants remain the same.   It was a
change in those habits, at the period, which led to the
abandonment of Gothic architecture.   Modified, it is
true, is the Italian school in more northern climates,
inasmuch as in Southern Europe, the open galleries
and colonnades that are practised, are necessary for the
introduction of breezes which it is a main object in
more northern climates to exclude.   In short, the forms
and combinations in all styles of architecture are but
so many means of suiting the climate and country in
which they are used; and the very styles of Schinkel
and Klenze, who are the heroes of the reviewer, are
founded upon the Italian school, filtered through that
of France, now the most intelligent in Europe, as will
hereafter be shown.   Does the reviewer suppose that
the introduction of a few *antefixæ*, with a mixture of
foliage and volutes with honeysuckles and semi-animals,
makes a Grecian design?   *Parva leves capiunt animos.*
It is not by a profusion of Greek forms and ornaments
that the architect catches the spirit of Grecian design,
for they may be so applied, though in themselves highly

* Foreign Quarterly Review, No. xxvii.

beautiful, as to become objects of absurdity.*   Many
of the ornaments so profusely lavished over the surfaces
of the works of Borromini, are in themselves exceedingly beautiful.   It is their application and propriety
as respects the design, and their consonance with the
whole, which not only enhance the value of ornaments,
but that also of the building to which they are applied.
So of orders and buildings; of which latter, the circular temple of Tivoli seems an instance so strong, that
one may almost say a fac-simile of it in a dissimilar
situation would lose its effect; certain it is, that the
order used in it, which has been more than once applied in the metropolis, *there* loses all its original
charms.   It was in this adaptation of certain forms and
orders to certain situations that the antients so greatly
excelled.   The same sort of feeling produced the magnificent street architecture of Rome, of Florence, and
of the other cities of Italy, in which the reviewer
discovers nothing but " *prettinesses and puerilities.*"†

It seems, notwithstanding the vast destruction
which the Goths occasioned in Italy, from sufficient
remains that could not but have existed, reasonable to
conclude, that the earliest palaces in Italy, after the
revival of the arts, must have partaken in some
measure of the arrangement and design of the palaces
of antient Rome, which, beyond question, were as
different from the houses of the Greeks, as were the
customs of the two countries.   Pompeii furnishes no

* As are the victories *applied where triglyphs should have been in the
Wachtgebäude at Berlin,—objects which are much lauded by the reviewer.*

† Foreign Quarterly Review, No. xxvii.

clue either to the plan or elevation of a Roman house.
" Scalis habito tribus sed altis,"* gives a notion as to
height, which under Augustus, was limited to seventy
feet. The great court yard was then a feature, as it
still is, in the palaces of Italy, and there can be little
doubt that the modern palaces are not very dissimilar
to the edifices of antient Rome, making sufficient
allowance for change of habits. In how many things,
agricultural for instance, may the similarity between
the antient and modern practices of Italy be traced?
Is it not then allowable to assume that the modern is
very much founded on the model of the antient buildings? If it be not so, the greater is the respect due to
those illustrious architects who designed and executed
the Italian palaces of the fifteenth and sixteenth
centuries, which have been the foundation, in point of
arrangement, of all modern edifices, into which com-
forts have been gradually introduced, suitable to higher
civilisation, and dependant on the customs of the
people. To the Greeks, at all events, we are not
indebted for these : our debt to them is limited to the
application of Grecian Doric columns to modern
buildings, to which, however beautiful in their original
application, they are, from circumstances now totally
inapplicable, nay, even in their application, altogether
obviously absurd. The mere mention of the obstruc-
tion of light and heat in this climate, and that of
France and Northern Germany, is sufficient to show

* Martial 1, 118.
† Trajan afterwards limited them to sixty feet.

how inapplicable is the style, which twenty years ago was so rife in this country, but which is now, happily, if one may judge from the practice of the French and British architects, fast decreasing.

Three distinct styles may be traced in the Italian school of architecture ; or perhaps the general school may be said to have three subdivisions ; the Florentine, the Roman, and the Venetian. I shall begin with some remarks relative to the first.

Every one is aware that, owing to climate, habits of the people, and the materials that are at hand in different districts, different styles of building are adopted, which may be termed local. Indeed the materials alone frequently govern the architect, or at least considerably influence the lightness or massiveness of the style adopted. Tuscany furnishes quarries, from which enormous blocks of stone may be extracted, close to the surface. This circumstance might in some measure account for the solid, solemn, and monotonous masses which form one of the characteristic features of the Florentine school. In what survives of the ruins of ancient Etruria, the same colossal species of construction appears to corroborate the conjecture. To this must be added another circumstance, not of less account, namely, the necessity of affording defence to a nobility in a place where insurrection was continually occurring. The palaces of the Medici, the Pitti and the Strozzi, appear almost equally calculated for a siege, and the purposes of a palace. The style seems rigorously to forbid the use of columns in the exterior, whence cor-

nices of stupendous height and projection seem not to
be misplaced. The courts, however, are generally
surrounded by columns, and from the exterior little
notion could be formed of the interior distribution.
I cannot, however, refrain from calling the attention
of the student to the cornices employed by the Florentine school, inasmuch as there is no member of a building from which it receives so great an assistance and
effect as from the cornice. In the best and most
celebrated examples, such as the Strozzi and Pandolfini palaces, and the Picolomini palace at Siena,
whose court and staircase are of extraordinary beauty,
the cornice is proportioned to the whole height of the
building, as the height of an order, notwithstanding
the horizontal subdivisions and small cornices that
occur between the ground and the crowning members.
Not less celebrated than those just mentioned, is that
of the Farnese palace at Rome, which has always been
considered one of the most powerful architectural efforts
of Michael Angelo.

Without allusion to the double cupola which
Brunelleschi raised at Florence, the first of its species,
and without doubt the prototype of St. Peter's, and a
host of others, the churches at Florence do not so well
exhibit the principles and character of the school
which owes its origin to that city, as its palaces. Yet
they possess great interest, as models on which the
Roman school developed the striking features found,
with different degrees of purity, in all the great modern
churches of Europe. The plans of the Duomo, of

the churches of S. Michele, Sta. Maddelena, S. Pancrazio, S. Lorenzo, and S. Spirito, are the key to all excellence in modern art, as respects real church architecture.* Unfortunately the churches of this school are, even at the present day, in few instances finished, the façades being generally imperfect.

The celebrity of the Florentine school is not dependent on its churches and palaces alone. One of the most beautiful works, as well for design as science in construction, the bridge "*della Santissima Trinità*," at Florence, in which a maximum of water-way was obtained for the waters of the Arno, combined with a beauty of form unappreciable by any graphic means, still remains to attest the consummate skill of Ammanati.

In considering the greatness of the architects of Florence, it ought to be kept in mind, that principally to them was Europe indebted for the revival of the arts, and that the names of Giotto, Arnolfo di Lapo, and Cimabue, must be added to the catalogue of illustrious names recorded in the history of the arts in that city. The period of the Florentine school, which began with Brunelleschi, includes Michellozzo, Leo. Bat. Alberti, Cronaca, the architect of the Strozzi palace, which has been just mentioned, Raffaelle Sanzio, Benedetto da Maiano, Baccio d'Agnolo, Baccio Bandinelli, Buontalenti, and Ammanati, and extends from A.D. 1400 to about 1600. For the purpose of comparing it with

* The reader must not suppose that the species of church architecture here alluded to, is that whereof the commissioners for building churches in England, where packing people in them seems the principal object, have the remotest idea.

the works of the other schools, and in order to distinguish its peculiar character and features, the Palazzo Pandolfini, and the Palazzi Strozzi and Pitti, may be taken. They will sufficiently illustrate to the student the principles of design involved in their composition. Michael Angelo, though a Florentine, and some others, such as Sangallo, have been classed among its architects, their works partaking more of the character of the Roman school, on which I shall now proceed to say a few words.

Though Rome, during the period of the rise and progress of its school of architecture, was not exempt from insurrectionary troubles, the style of its palaces is far less massive than that of Florence. None of its buildings have the fortress-like appearance of those in the last-named city. They partake of a lightness and grace which indicate more pacific habits on the part of the people, and an advancing state of the art from a better acquaintance with the models of antiquity, which were close at hand. The introduction of columns is frequent, and great pains and study appear to have been always bestowed on the elevations of their buildings, in many of them, indeed, so much so, that they masque but indifferent interiors. The entrance is almost invariably converted into a principal feature, and frequently, though abuses are not uncommon in its composition, with great success. The court is usually surrounded with an arcade, from which a staircase of great dimensions leads to the *sala* of the palace. The general character is, that of grandeur, divested of the severity that marks the Florentine school.   Of all the private palaces of Europe, Rome possesses the noblest example in the Farnese Palace. *   This edifice forms a quadrangle of 256 feet by 185 feet.   It is constructed of brick, with the exception of the dressings of the doors and windows, and the quoins of the fronts, the entablature and the loggia in the Strada Giulia, which are of Travertine stone. †   The interior of the court is of the same sort of stone, and is beautifully wrought.   The elevation consists of three stories, including the ground floor, separated by impost cornices.   The only interruption to the symmetry and simplicity is, the loggia in the centre of the first story, which is connected with the windows on each side of it by four columns.   The window dressings to the ground story are square headed and extremely simple ; to the next floor they are flanked by columns bearing entablatures, crowned with triangular and circular pediments alternately, and the third story has circular headed windows, and the pediments in this are all triangular.   These last are by no means in so good taste as the preceding, though

* " Ce vaste palais Farnese, qui a tout prendre, pour la grandeur de la masse, la regularite de son ensemble, et l'excellence de son architecture, a tenu jusqu'ici, dans l'opinion des artistes, le premier rang entre tous les palais qu'on renomme." Quat. de Quincy.   Vie de San Gallo.

† This stone is quarried in several parts of Italy.   It is difficult to work for sculpture; hence Vasari says of it—" Ma più d'ogni altro Maestro, hà nobilitata questa pietra Michelagnolo Buonaroti nell' ornamento del cortile di casa Farnese, havendovi con maraviglioso giudizio fatto d'essa pietra far finestre, Maschere Mensole e tante altre simili bizarrie, lavorate tutte come si fà il marmo, che non si può veder alcuno altro simile ornamento piu bello."

it is probable they were by Michael Angelo, who
added the cornice, whereof Vasari observes—" è stu-
pendissimo il cornicione maggiore del medesimo
palazzo nella facciata dinanzi, non si potendo alcuna
cosa ne più bella ne più magnifica desiderare." The façade towards the Strada Giulia differs from the others
in the centre only, in which there are three stories of
arcades, to the loggia, of three arches each, with
columns of the Doric order on their piers in the lower
story, and of the Ionic and Corinthian orders in the
other stories, corresponding in form and dimensions
with the three ranks of arcades in the court.   It is
probable that this central feature was not in the
original design of San Gallo, but was introduced at
the time of completing the third story.   Magnificent
as is the exterior of the palace, from its symmetry and
simplicity, the interior is not less so.   The quadrangular
court is eighty-eight feet wide between the columns of
the arcades, which reign through two of the stories
only, the third being a solid wall thereover, pierced
with windows.   But all description must fall short
in conveying an adequate idea of the edifice.   " C'est
un edifice toujours digne," says de Quincy, " d'être le
sejour d'un prince."   The Palace at S. Giovanni
Laterano, is another beautiful specimen of the Roman
school, and is the work of Fontana, but into any details of it I have not space to enter.   The two are fair
examples to illustrate the Roman school in the pala-
tial style of architecture.   The Villas, the *ocelli
d'Italia*, round the suburbs of Rome, are far lighter in

style than the buildings of which we have just been
speaking; to these we are indebted for all the beauty
of plan which is found in the modern country houses
of this country.   The riches and taste of a few cardi-
nals studded the environs of the eternal city, though
a few are within the city, with some of the most refined specimens of the art.   But I must proceed to
notice the churches in which the Roman school was
super-eminent.

It will, for the purpose of giving the reader the
requisite information on the Roman churches, be
scarcely necessary to refer him to more than the
church of St. Peter's, in which examples of the school
in all its stages may be found ; and this church is so
well known by representations, that I shall not make
any remarks upon it, further than that it was left by
Michael Angelo, though unfinished, a stupendous
monument of his gigantic genius.   How far the
lengthening the foot of the cross by Carlo Maderno
was an act of bad taste, I am not prepared to decide.
Internally, I do not, as most of the critics, think
its effect was injured, but externally, the church was
completely ruined.   That Maderno was a sad bungler,
there is no doubt, for the arches nearer the door are
smaller than the others, and to crown his other errors,
the part which he added to the nave is not in a continued line with the other work, but inclines considerably on the plan to the south, so much so, as to strike
every educated eye.   Besides this, his taste was exceedingly bad.

Most of the churches of Rome are very similar in plan, consisting of a nave and side aisles (with chapels in the latter) separated by arcades. Frequently a dome is introduced over the intersection of the nave with the transepts, in which latter are usually the chapels of the Virgin and of the Holy Sacrament. The choir generally terminates in a semi-circle. Unlike the churches of the Florentine school, the interiors of those of Rome are decorated to excess. One very great abuse in them, which constantly occurs, is, the practice of masking them with false fronts or façades, so that there is no connection between the architecture of the exterior and that of the interior. In very many cases the sides are hidden by adjoining buildings, so that they are completely lost to the eye, and this circumstance may have very much conduced to the repetition of the abuse. Faulty, however, as these edifices are, compared with the best examples of their palaces, Europe is indebted to them as models, which in more modern times have been much purified. Abuse was carried to its height by Borromini, and yet the Borrominesque style became so fashionable, that a city in Europe can scarcely be named in which its *bizarreries* are not recorded. Borromini founded a school of his own, which must not be confounded with the Roman one to disgrace it; and as there are less materials for variety of style in architecture than in the other arts, he proved the maxim, that when an architect acquires such a manner as to lead one to the notion that he invented it, he has only fallen on novelty, and novelty in architecture is generally caprice.

The Roman school was founded by Bramante—it includes the names San Gallo, M. A. Buonaroti, Sanso-vino a scholar of Bramante, Vignola, and many others, ending in Domenico Fontana, and extending from about 1470 to 1607, a period of 130 years and upwards.

The Venetian school is characterised by its great lightness and elegance, the convenience it exhibits in distribution, and the abundant, perhaps exuberant, display of columns, pilasters, and arcades, in its composition. It seems to bear great analogy to its sister school of painting, and, like it, appears more calculated to address the senses with effect than the two preceding: and yet the analogy does not strictly hold in respect of its great purity. Venice was early in the field of art. In the twelfth century the church of St. Mark was commenced; and thenceforward, as the republic rose by its arms and commerce, its arts were destined to an equally brilliant career. Doubtless, the possession in its provinces of some fine monuments of antiquity, and its early communication with Greece, tended materially to the advancement of its architecture. That species of luxury which springs from the desire of individuals to perpetuate their name by their habitations, though, in general. it may not lead to works on a colossal scale, leads in a democracy (such were the States of Venice) to a more general diffusion of moderately splendid and elegant palaces. Hence, the very great number of beautiful

E

specimens of the building art which the Venetian school supplies.

San Micheli, who was born in 1484, may with propriety be called its founder. He visited Rome at the early age of sixteen for the study of the ancient monuments of the art in that city, in which he was employed on several important commissions, and after many years returned to his native country. The mode in which he combined pure and beautiful architecture with the requirements of fortifications, is to be seen and admired at Verona, where the *Porta del Pallio* shews his extraordinary ingenuity and taste. His most admired works are his palaces at Verona; though, perhaps, the palace Grimani, at Venice, is his most magnificent work. San Micheli never copied himself, but his general style of composition is with a basement of rustic work, whereon is raised an order, frequently with arched windows, in which he much delighted, and which were connected with the order in the manner of an arcade, the whole being crowned with the proper entablature. The genius of San Micheli, in architecture, was of the highest class ; his works are conspicuous for their excellent construction, convenience, unity, harmony, and simplicity, which threw into shade the little abuses into which he occasionally fell: by Michael Angelo he was held in great esteem, and he is an admirable example in his compositions for the student. The military architecture in use to this day owes its origin to San Micheli, though Vauban and his school have usually borne the credit of it. Sansovino, to whom the Roman school might lay claim, if the works on which he was engaged at Rome, and not his style, would alone justify it, is well known and esteemed as the architect of the library of St. Mark, at Venice, a building, however, wherein many improprieties are to be found. Though Sansovino was a contemporary of San Micheli, he does not appear to have profited by the same exemplars as that architect; he was, nevertheless, a great master of his art. The library of St. Mark, just mentioned, is of noble design. It consists of two orders, a highly ornamented Doric, and above a graceful Ionic. Of both these orders the entablatures are inordinately lofty; the latter was so set out for the purpose of exhibiting the series of beautiful sculptures with which it is decorated. Over the cornice is a balustrade, whose piers the ablest scholars of Sansovino ornamented with statues. On the ground floor a portico is raised three steps from the level of the piazza, consisting of twenty one arches, supported by pilasters, or piers, decorated with columns. Arches are formed in the interior answering to the external ones, sixteen of which, with their internal apartments, are used for shops. The centre arch conducts to a magnificent staircase leading to the hall, beyond which is the library. Though it has many faults, the library of St. Mark is remarkable for its grace and elegance, and is, perhaps, the chef-d'œuvre of the master. Sansovino, whilst engaged on it, proposed the following problem, " How can the exact half of a metope be so contrived as to make it fall in the angle of a Doric frieze." The solution, as practised in this building, however, is a bungling absurdity, namely, lengthening the frieze just so much as is necessary to make out the deficiency. So great was the esteem of the Venetians for Titian and Sansovino, that on an extraordinary tax being imposed by the senate they were specially exempted from the payment of it.

Until a late review* and some minor critics appeared, no doubt was ever entertained in the world of art on the rank in it which Palladio has had assigned to him, nor will the reader easily be led to believe, that an amateur reviewer of the nineteenth century has issued, for the instruction of the public, the following rich display of his utter want of knowledge on the subject. " Far better would it be," quoth the reviewer, " to emancipate ourselves at once from classical precedents, than to adopt a wavering, indefinite course—one that injudiciously challenges immediate comparison, by pointing to professed models, and so forcing into notice the discrepancies ingrafted upon them; greatly, therefore, do WE prefer many specimens of the *ante-reformed* architecture of Italy, if we may so term it—when, although circular arches and columns appear, even the latest Roman style was entirely lost sight of, and one altogether different substituted for it—*to the productions of the Palladian school, which seem, for the most part,* BLUNDERING COPIES, UNDERTAKEN IN UTTER IGNO-

* Foreign Quarterly, No. xxix.

RANCE *of the works from which they pretend to be derived.*" Unawed by the reviewer's condemnation of the Palladian school, fortified by the concurring testimony of all the artists of celebrity that have existed since the time of Palladio, in opposition to that of the reviewer, and satisfied, as Hooker says, " that such is the final victory of all truth, that they which have not the hearts to love her, acknowledge, that to hate her they have no cause," I shall now proceed to a short notice of this architect, who, by grace and elegance of proportion in his works, by a consummate knowledge of harmony in their distribution, by the use of columns never called in to his aid, but to fortify and support, produced combinations unknown to the antients, and beauty of which they might have been justly proud.

The interior distribution of the palaces and villas of Palladio, in respect of plan, would, without considerable change, be but ill-suited to modern habits. Convenience changes as the mode of life varies—indeed, except in a private building of large extent, which in this country rarely falls to the lot of an architect to execute, the large quadrangular court which is constant throughout Italy, is itself a thing unknown. His plans, however, are convenient, considering the people for whom they were executed, and must be judged of only as far as they go. With his eyes constantly turned to the practice and detail of the antients, Palladio acquired a bold, simple, and agreeable style; and, except in his churches, the beauties of Palladio are to be sought in his façades, and the quadrangles of his palaces. Pedestals, either with panels or raisings, were always avoided by him; his architraves were rarely sculptured, and the upper ornaments of his entablatures were always centered above each other. His doors, windows, and niches are composed with much simplicity, and if crowned with pediments are unbroken. In the members of his cornices he never lost sight of the character of the order employed, and was extremely particular in the due adjustment of its profiles. He did not, however, scruple to vary the proportions of an order according to the nature of the building to which it was applied; and in the proportions of his churches and apartments, he seems to have delighted, as did our Wren after him, in arithmetical, geometrical, and harmonic proportions. Though he seems to have been particularly partial to the use of the Ionic order, in which he has always made two faces to the capital, yet he did not unfrequently use each of the others. His Corinthian capital is not, however, among the beauties of his practice. The domes which he erected are almost invariably hemispherical. It is not to be supposed that his buildings are perfect, though they certainly approach perfection; but it is probable that many of the abuses that are to be seen in them arose either from want of sufficient superintendence, the great number he designed being very great, or were introduced after his death, the instructions in his work on architecture being very peremptory on the subject of abuses.* So well based

* Milizia Vita di Palladio.

upon the practice of the ancients does the style of
Palladio seem to have been, that it is, with the necessary modifications, suited to all nations, and such as
the ancients themselves would have adopted. Fuseli,
speaking of the gigantic powers of Michael Angelo,
says the "beggar rose from his hand the patriarch
of poverty," and it is with similar feeling and truth
that Le Grand says, "les fermes que dirigeait Palladio
et qu'il convrait de tuiles ou d'un chaume rustique,
l'emportent de beaucoup sur les palais somptueux de
Borromini, ou sur les riches et bizarres productions de
Guarino Guarini."   There is indeed no question that
simplicity, unity, and style are more powerful ingredients in producing grandeur, than great volume or
large masses.

The number of palaces and villas with which
Palladio enriched the Venetian and Vicentine ter-
ritories is almost incredible ; in them the variety of
plan, as well as elevation, seems as inexhaustible as
their number. "Even when obliged," says * Forsyth,
"to contend with the coarsest Gothic at La Ragione,
how skilfully has Palladio screened the external bar-
barisms of that reversed hulk, by a Greek '(Roman)'
elevation as pure as the original would admit !   His
Vicentine villas have been often imitated in England,
and are models more adapted to resist both our climate
and our reasoning taste, than the airy, extravagant

* Remarks on Antiquities, Arts, and Letters, during an Excursion in Italy.
Forsyth has some strange notions ; but his taste may be much more depended
on than the Reviewer's.

structures of the south." Of the private buildings of this great master, I would refer the student to the Palazzo Thiene at Vicenza, which, though unfinished, sufficiently exhibits the design; to the villa Capra, in the neighbourhood of Vicenza, and the Carità at Venice. Of his public buildings, to the church of the Redeemer in the last named city; each of them surpassing all others of their kind, and exhibiting in an illustrative manner the great versatility of the master. The exterior of his churches are generally faulty. The two half pediments in the church of the Redeemer, and one or two others, are abuses of which it is scarcely possible to think he would have been guilty. Palladio did not attain to that age to which it was the lot of so many great masters of olden times to arrive, being only sixty-two at the time of his death. "The public and posterity," says Milizia, "have awarded him the fame which his various works so nobly merit." Inigo Jones and Lord Burlington seem to have been in this country of the Venetian school, whilst Wren appears to have practised more on the principles of the Roman school. Vincenzo Scamozzi was the last architect of the Venetian school who attained great celebrity. The son of an architect, and born in a country which had in his time become the nursery of architecture, he exhibited his power at a very early age. Like Palladio, and other great architects, he selected for his principal guides the antiquities of Rome, and the precepts of Vitruvius, who was then "the chief stone of the corner," but in these wise days of reviewers, and makers of national galleries, is "the stone which the builders have refused." There can be no doubt he profited by observation of the works of Palladio, which must in his youth have been carrying on at Venice with great vigour, though he affected occasionally to decry the edifices of that master. Notwithstanding the opinion of De Quincy,[*] that Scamozzi was formed by the examples of Palladio, it appears to me, that his style is more founded on that of San Micheli, or Sansovino. It is not, however, necessary to discuss this point; certain it is that he must have possessed great natural talents, for at a very early period of his career we find him employed by the canons of San Salvadore in opening the lantern to the cupola of their church, in which task it appears he acquitted himself with great ability. The upper order of the Procurazie Nuove, respecting which he has often been reproached for not confining himself to two stories, so as to complete the design of Sansovino, is one of the most beautiful pieces of composition in Italy; and there can be but one opinion on this head— that if the whole of the Piazza San Marco had been from the continued design of Scamozzi, it would have placed in the background every other Piazza in Europe. The two lower stories of the Procurazie Nuove are similar in design to the library of Saint Mark. It is much to be regretted that Scamozzi had not time to attend to the execution of the whole of the work whereof we are speaking, which would have consisted of

* Vie de Scamozzi.

thirty-nine arcades, whose length would have extended
to four hundred and twenty-six feet.   Scamozzi only
superintended the first thirteen, the three which were
built by Sansovino excepted; the remainder were
trusted to the care of builders rather than artists, and
discover, from the little attention bestowed upon pre-
serving the profiles, a negligence indicating decline in
the arts at Venice.   But the work which places Scamozzi in the first rank as an architect, is the cathedral
at Salzburg, whither he was invited by the arch-
bishop of that see.   This church, which was not
finished till after his death in 1616, is four hundred
and fifty-four feet long, and three hundred and twenty-
nine feet wide; its plan being a Latin cross, whose
centre is crowned by a cupola : the interior is planned
with a nave, and two side-aisles, the former whereof
is sixty-four feet wide, and one hundred and seven feet
high.   The employ of Scamozzi seems to have been
universal, and his country have to lament that he did
not confine himself to fewer commissions, in which
case his works would have been more perfect and
worthier of his great name ; for it is quite certain that
no one can carry a work into execution so well as he
who designed it.

The Venetian school contains the names of very
few architects more than those we have named; they
seem to have monopolised the whole employ of the
states and neighbourhood of Venice for the period of
about 110 years, ending in 1616.   But, though not
longer destined to flourish in the soil where it was

first planted, its scions. grafted in other countries spread their branches throughout Europe, and prospered wherever they extended.

As the French and English schools—for no other nation in Europe had any, the Spanish perhaps excepted—were founded on those of Italy, but on that especially which I have last considered, I think it may be advantageous to make a few observations on them by way of conclusion to this section.   The earliest architect in France who may be said to have had a perception of Italian architecture, was Jean Bullant, between 1543 and 1573.   From a portico in the castle of St. Ecouen, he appears to have preceded the age in which he lived to such a degree, that he must be considered the harbinger of good taste in France.

The wars in Italy under Charles VIII., Louis XII., and Francis I., had made the French intimately acquainted with the works of Italy, and the taste of the last named monarch particularly induced him to bring from that country some of their most celebrated artists, so that there was almost a colony of them in France.   Amongst these was Vignola, who was many years resident in the country; and this may with some probability account for the great esteem in which that great master's profiles have always been held in France, and indeed I may say, in which they are still held, though in other respects the French is rather founded on the Venetian school.   Another architect of note, Sebastian Serlio, was engaged in the country by Francis, and died there. Buildings are to be judged of relatively as well as abstractedly; hence the opportunities of every class which the period afforded must be taken into consideration before the powers and merits of an architect can be properly appreciated. In this respect, Lescot's works at the Louvre are entitled to great praise. He was the cotemporary of Jean Gougeon, the architect of the well known and admired Fountain of the Innocents, at Paris, which lost much of its beauty, when, many years ago, it was taken down and its site changed. From the works of Bullant, Lescot, and Gougeon, the progress of pure architecture, one might have supposed, would have been without check till it reached that point to which it had been carried in Italy. Such, however, was far from being the case. Mary de Medicis, who was a native of Florence, but afterwards a resident in France, anxious, when she was about to build the Luxembourg palace, to have it designed in a manner which would remind her of her native city, made her architect, De Brosse, adopt a style, as nearly as circumstances would allow, resembling the palaces of Tuscany. The rustic work of the Pitti palace seems to have been uppermost in the mind of the architect; but his version of it is a failure. In Florence, the palaces are on so gigantic a scale, that they can bear out the rustic and embossed work employed upon them; but when reduced in size, a building in which they are used allows but sparing use of these practices. This palace became a model

for the fashion of the day, and produced an intermediate style which lasted many years in France, and
arrested the advances to perfection whereof the above
works of Bullant and others gave promise. De Brosse
was, however, an able artist, and well knew how to
group his masses so as to produce great effect. His
last work, the acqueduct of Arcueil, was finished in
1624, and it is supposed he did not long survive its
completion.

Under Louis the XIV. the art remained, for the
most part, in the intermediate state I have just noticed, notwithstanding the great efforts he made to
embellish the kingdom with its productions. He sent
for Bernini to design the additions and alterations
contemplated at the Louvre, and it was a happy thing
for France that this high and haughty architect was
disgusted with the workmen of Paris, and returned to
Italy without executing his designs; for grand as they
were, in respect of dimensions, they were exceedingly
corrupt in composition.* But there is a still weightier
reason why France had reason to rejoice in their re-
jection, which is, that it gave Perrault an opportunity
of ornamenting their capital with one of the most
splendid monuments of art that Europe can boast;
one which changed the heavy style, then in vogue, and
gave the French artists that impulse whose power is
still in action upon them. The beauties of the façade
of the Louvre so completely overpower its defects, that I
can hardly bring myself to the mention of its coupled

* The reader may refer to them in Durand's *Parallele des Edifices.*

columns, and the arch of the central door rising into
the story of the colonnade.   It seems to be the fate of
architects to fall under the lash of poets.   Ben Jon-
son lampooned Inigo Jones in his Bartholomew Fair,
under the title of Lantern Leatherhead; Pope and
Vanbrugh did not very well agree.   So Perrault,
whose first profession was that of medicine, which,
however, he only practised for his friends and the
poor, having spoken ill of one of Boileau's satires,
was told by the poet that " *de mechant medecin de-
vient bon architecte.*"   Perrault competed in this
work with Le Vau, the king's principal architect,
against whom, and others, he was successful; he was,
however, assisted in the execution, as it is said, by
that artist, though, from Perrault's intimate acquaintance with the several branches of science, one can
scarcely believe the assistance was necessary.   Cotemporary with Perrault was Le Mercier, the architect
of the church of St. Roch, in the Rue St. Honorè, at
Paris, who followed, but with much originality, the precepts and principles of the Venetian school, and died in
1660, twenty-eight years before the decease of Perrault.

Mansart, the architect of Versailles, and an
especial favorite of Louis XIV., had amazing employ
between 1675, and his death in 1708.   He was, in
every respect, a disciple of the Venetian school.   His
plan of the church and dome of the Invalids at Paris,
is exceedingly well composed: the latter is, perhaps,
the third or fourth in rank of domes that have obtained great reputation.   De Quincy observes of it,

that, though nothing which can be called classic is to
be noticed about it, yet it contains nothing offensive
to the principles of the art. It is a whole, in which
richness and elegance are combined, in which lightness and solidity are well balanced, in which unity is
not injured by variety, and whose general effect silences
the critic, however he may be disposed to find fault.
In Versailles, the taste which was, as we have above
noticed, introduced by De Brosse, prevails ; but the
interior of the chapel affords a noble example of what
this artist was capable. His relation and pupil, Jacques
Ange Gabriel, was worthy the master. The colonnades to the Garde-meuble in the Place Louis XV.
exhibit a style which, with the exception of Perrault's
façade, not all the patronage of Louis XIV. could
elicit. For the renewal of good taste in France, that
nation is under a debt of gratitude to Gabriel. He
has been accused of pirating the Louvre; and, till reflection and comparison are bestowed on his work,
some ground for the charge may appear to exist.
The difference, however, between the two works is
great. The basement of Perrault is a wall pierced
with windows ; that of Gabriel, an arcade. In the
upper story the columns are not coupled, which is the
case in Perrault's work. These two circumstances
alone change the character of Gabriel's work, so as
to free him from the imputation. The great extent
of the Place Louis XV. is injurious to the effect of
this, or perhaps, from the street in the centre, one
would with greater propriety say, these buildings.

Antoine, the architect of the mint at Paris, continued
the style whereof we are speaking; and though the age
of Louis XV. could not boast of stupendous edifices,
like those of Louis le Grand, it exhibited a better and
far purer taste. This architect was the first who
made use of the Greek Doric in France, known there
by the work of Le Roy ; but it has long since fallen
into disuse in that country.* Antoine died in 1801.

A vow of Louis XV., during a dangerous illness,
added to the extensive commissions with which Soufflot
was charged about the middle of the eighteenth century, by his employment on the church of St. Gene-
viève, or, as it was afterwards called, the Pantheon at
Paris, the largest modern church in France, and
second to none in simplicity, elegance, and variety.
The great hospital at Lyons had deservedly brought
this architect into notice, and out of a great number
of competitors the design of Soufflot was adopted. Its
plan is a species of Greek cross, and the interior is separated into three very unequal parts by isolated columns,
instead of the usual Italian plan of arches, yet both
internally and externally it is strictly of the Venetian
school. Of the interior, the light effect produced by

* It was used at L'Hospice de la Charité. Quatremère de Quincy makes the
following observations on it in his Memoir of Antoine. " Ce Petit monument
le premier du style dorique grec exécuté a Paris, est un des ouvrages qui firent
le plus remarquer le talent d'Antoine, par les artistes et les gens de goût.
Sans doute cet essai eût continué d'attirer attention si, au lieu d'une heureuse
emulation entre les architectes et d'une application judicieuse aux monumens aux
quels convient le caractère de cet ordre, une sort de courant de mode n'en
eût fait un emploi banal, sans mesure sans discernement aucun, aux edifices les
plus vulgaires, et jusqu'à en rendre l'aspect insignifiant et même fastidieux."

the columns is pleasing, though it has justly been objected that some of them have no office to perform. Objection has also been made to the width of the intercolumniations of the portico, and other parts, on which this is not the proper place to dwell. Notwithstanding all the criticisms, however, it is a magnificent edifice.   Its greatest fault was instability about the great piers of the dome, which gave Soufflot great uneasiness, and is said to have hastened his death. The failure was rectified by his pupil Rondelet, who, with great skill, gave perfect security to the building.   Soufflot died in 1781, at the age of sixty-eight years.

Gondouin was another of the celebrated architects of the French school of this period.   His veneration for the works of Palladio was so unbounded, that he performed a second journey into Italy almost for their study exclusively.   Indeed, at this time the heavy style of Louis XIV. was quite extinct, and that of the Venetian school every where prevalent.   It is in Paris that the most beautiful street architecture is to be found, excepting some few cities of Italy. So great are the French in this respect, that the education of an architect cannot be considered complete until he has made acquaintance with the examples it affords.   He will spend his time much more advantageously in this capital than in the pilgrimages to Berlin and Munich, recommended by the reviewer in the Foreign Quarterly, who has hereinbefore been noticed.

Previous to the revival of the arts in Italy, the

practice of pointed architecture in England had
flourished as much as it had on the continent; and in
that and the Tudor style, up to the reign of Henry
VIII., the skill and talents displayed by the English
architects and freemasons, were not inferior to those
exhibited in the buildings of similar character in
France and Germany, though it must be conceded
ours were on a much smaller scale.   Sir Horatio Pal-
lavicini, a Genoese, who made some figure in this
country in the reign of Elizabeth, was the first who
erected a house in this kingdom in the Italian style,
as it is called, it being of course, from the little study
bestowed upon it at that time, very much debased.
This house was at Little Shelford, in Essex, and it is
a matter for regret, that it was taken down in 1754.
During the sixteenth and seventeenth centuries, the
only architects whose names have reached our time
are those of John Thorpe, Gerard Christmas, Thomas
Holte (who built the schools at Oxford, in which,
though the parts are all bad, yet the grandeur of the
court is considerable, and the whole indicates a return to classical architecture), and Rodolph Symonds.
Thorpe built Burleigh House, and was much engaged
by the nobility of the time.   The late Sir John
Soane possessed a curious collection of his drawings,
in folio, among which is the design of a house proposed for himself, in the form, as to plan, of the
initials of his name, thus :—I⫟T the I and the
T being joined by a passage which led to the offices,
which are in the I.   Wollaton Hall, in Nottingham-

shire, was by Thorpe and Smithson.   Its composition, as a whole, is worthy of far better detail than
they could give it, from the want of intimate acquaintance with classical architecture, which it is probable
they only knew from the wood blocks of the books on
architecture then extant in England.   A certain John
of Padua, seems also about this time to have ex-
ercised the art here with considerable success, having
been employed by the Protector Somerset for his
palace in the Strand in 1549.

In the reign of James I. the passion for large
houses seems to have been even greater than it was
in the time of Elizabeth.   Among the most considerable of them, in point of extent, was that at Campden,
in Glocestershire, burnt down during the civil wars.
It was quadrangular, with the garden front towards a
grand terrace.   The flanks projected, with large bay
windows.   In the centre was a portico carried up
with the five orders of architecture, and thereunder
an open corridor.   The parapet was capriciously furnished with pediments, and the chimneys were made
to assume the shape of twisted columns, surmounted
by Corinthian capitals.   On the roof was a large
dome which was nightly illuminated for guiding
travellers on their way.   The whole building was
decorated with highly enriched entablatures.   Thus,
by degrees, the art approached a perfection which
was very soon afterwards realised.

The reigns of James and Charles I., and particularly that of the latter, were favorable to the arts

generally, but particularly so to that which is the subject of these pages. Walpole thus introduces to the notice of his readers the architect of the banqueting house at Whitehall. " The last artist that I have to produce of this period, but the greatest in his profession, that has appeared in these kingdoms, and so great, that in that reign of arts we scarce know the name of another architect, was Inigo Jones, who, if a table of fame, like that in the Tatler, were to be formed for men of real and indisputable genius in every country, would save England from the disgrace of not having her representative among the arts. Vitruvius* drew up his grammar, Palladio shewed him the practice, Rome displayed a theatre worthy of his emulation, and king Charles was ready to encourage, employ, and reward his talents. This is the history of Inigo Jones." It is scarcely credible that the garden front at St. John's, Oxford, and the banqueting house, are from the designs of the same artist: the first borders on the Tudor style, and shews him struggling to emancipate himself from the trammels of early education ; the last exhibits him freed from his bonds, after the study of the works of the Venetian school, which he adopted as his model.

The banqueting house, a very minute part of the palace which Jones designed for our kings, would not

* It is curious in these later days to observe authors and critics treating this author with derision and contempt, because he has admitted into his valuable and interesting books on architecture some few fabulous and absurd tales. In the history of the early architects we find not one of eminence who did not make this author's work the subject of his constant study.

have yielded in extent or magnificence to any now
known or on record.   Its extent from north to south
would have been eleven hundred and 'fifty-two feet,
and from east to west eight hundred and forty feet,
covering a plot of upwards of twenty-two acres, and
containing seven courts.   His river front of Old
Somerset House, which was an exquisite specimen of
the Venetian school, was not surpassed by any of the
works of even San Micheli or Palladio. Jones died
about 1651.   His pupil and relation Webb succeeded
him; and some designs have been attributed to the
master, which in truth belong to the scholar, who
carried into execution the design made by Jones for
the Hospital at Greenwich.

That Inigo Jones had laid too solid a foundation
for his art in England to allow of its decay, if supplied
with the patronage of the country, was exemplified by
the works of Sir Christopher Wren, whose life was of
unusual duration, and who, through a very large portion of its course, was encountered by no rival. It is
unnecessary here to enumerate his works, which are
designed upon a style between the Venetian and
Roman schools. The faults and abuses, which are
many, in St. Paul's cathedral, the second in the world,
have been often discussed, and are therefore well
known; but its beauties so predominate as to entitle
Wren to a very high rank among the architects of
Europe. His church of St. Stephen's, Wallbrook,
equals, for beauty, lightness, and ingenious design, any
example of the Venetian school; and in this again it is

impossible to dwell upon the defects, so great are the merits which overbalance them. Wren died at the age of 91, in 1723.

Notwithstanding all the abuse that has been heaped upon Vanbrugh, who survived Wren but a few years, the extraordinary and picturesque mansion at Blenheim, which partakes considerably of the manner of Bernini, whilst it exists, will remain an honor to the country, and a monument of the great genius of its architect. Its merits were not lost on Sir Joshua Reynolds, who was among the first in later years to do justice to the talents of Vanbrugh. Had he depended on no better judges than Pope and Swift, and the rest of the critics of the day, his work would long since have been forgotten, and his name buried in oblivion. Price* says, " It appears to me that at Blenheim, Vanbrugh conceived and executed a very bold and difficult design—that of uniting in one building the beauty and magnificence of the Grecian" (Roman he should have said) " architecture, the picturesqueness of the Gothic, and the massive grandeur of a castle ; and that, in spite of many faults, for which he was justly reproached, he has formed in a style truly his own, and a well-combined whole, a mansion worthy of a great prince and warrior." Vanbrugh, who died in 1726, left no legitimate follower ; he formed no school, though Archer, who built Heythrop, and St. John's, Westminster, seems to have been ambitious in imitating him.

* In his Work on the Picturesque.

Hawksmoor, a pupil of Wren, if only for his church of St. Mary Woolnoth, in Lombard-street, must not be forgotten. It is a design evincing singular skill in adapting mass and detail to situation and aspect. Neither among the architects of this period must be omitted Henry Aldrich, D.D., dean of Christchurch, who died in 1710. He was a follower of the Venetian school, as is proved by his three sides of Peckwater-square at Oxford, and the garden front of Corpus Christi College, a façade which for correct taste is not surpassed by any edifice in Oxford. With him, but not equal to him, may be classed Dr. Clarke, one of the lords of the admiralty in the reign of Queen Anne, who built the library at Christchurch, and Sir James Burrough, master of Caius College, Cambridge, a triad of amateurs, who would have honoured any nation as professors of the art. Soon after these appeared another, who, amidst the high occupations of his station in society, and the gaieties of the circle in which he moved, found leisure to distinguish himself by a profound knowledge of architecture, and by the patronage of those artists who deserved it. The name of Lord Burlington will immediately occur to the reader.

Gibbs, a native of Scotland, met with extensive employ from about the year 1720, to his death in 1754. His portico of St. Martin's, as well as the body of the church, establish his claim to the patronage he received: not less does the interior of the Radcliffe Library, Oxford; whilst its dome, in a dis-

tant view of the city, connects with singular felicity
the different and varied public buildings of that
university.

Walpole says, that in the reign of George II.
architecture resumed all her rights; I am inclined to
think otherwise. The names of Flitcroft, Kent,
Campbell, and James, are the only ones that fill up the
gap till the appearance of Sir Robert Taylor and Sir
William Chambers, both men of splendid talents, and
both followers of the Venetian school, which, from its
aptitude to be modelled to our customs and habits, has
always been the adopted architecture of this country.
A further continuation of the history of architecture
in England would supply the names of many very
talented men; but the names of cotemporaries are
inadmissible.

On the first acquaintance of this country with
the works of Greece, through the publications of
Stuart and others, a style was engendered which is
now fast subsiding, and during the last fifteen years
the architecture of the country has considerably im-
proved; this may, however, be as much attributed to
our better acquaintance with the Italian school as to
any other cause. Had the late Mr. Nash, who was
beyond doubt a person of great taste, been enabled in
his youth to have seen the works of Palladio, and to
have studied them, I am confident that the new street
he formed would not have been exceeded in beauty by
many in Europe. As far as he understood it he was
a follower of the Venetian school; but his great

neglect of detail, and the little care he bestowed upon profiling his orders, arising from the deficiency of his early education as an architect, destroyed the effect of almost all his works.   His columns are sometimes outrageous in their proportions, and his cornices rarely much larger than decent sized copings.   He was heedless of propriety in the application of his orders ; and, from want of learning in his art, was unable to execute with any certainty the ideas of a very bold imagination.   In that of his villas, he was far more successful than in his street architecture.

SECTION IV.

GERMAN ARCHITECTURE.

No country in Europe exhibits such early and beautiful specimens of Romanesque and pointed architecture as are to be found in Germany.   The Rhine, and the southern parts, which were under the sway of the Romans, are the portions of it in which these examples are principally to be found.   The Christian religion, propagated from the East, introduced civilization and the arts of peace, the northern and eastern parts of central Europe being at the period of its introduction still involved in the gross darkness of Paganism.   The tenth and eleventh centuries produced the extraordinary cathedrals of Mentz and Worms,*with many others of Romanesque style, which still remain to attest the skill and taste of the German architects of that period. The forms of the plans of these edifices are clearly founded on the ancient basilicæ, being almost invariably composed of long naves with side aisles, transepts branching north and south from the eastern, and sometimes western end of the nave, at which a central tower usually rises above the other parts of the building; beyond this are placed the choir and the chancel terminated semi-circularly. It is true that in Italy a similar style had prevailed long enough to prove that it preceded that of the churches in Germany.

It is interesting, observes Dr. Moller,† to see in what a short space of time " the German architects discovered that the style they had adopted, which was formed upon a more southern one, was ill suited to their climate, and was replaced by one in which the high pitched roof and gable, and the almost consequent pointed arch, became prevalent." Before the minster at York had been thought of, Germany revelled in the display of the cathedrals at Cologne, Strasburgh, and St. Stephen's at Vienna, wherein the art had been carried to its highest perfections. This style in Germany, as elsewhere, was called into being

* It is highly gratifying to the antiquary and architect to observe the care bestowed in restoring these edifices, which is still in progress, particularly in the former, in which the author, on his visit last year, could perceive vast progress since that preceding.

† *Denkmahler der Deutschen Baukunst.*

by the circumstances of the times, whereof it was truly the offspring, and all the fostering which it may receive in the attempt to revive it in the present age, whether by individuals or governments, will be attended with failure and disgrace, unless, with it could be recalled the religious zeal and chivalric disposition of mankind which then prevailed. On this account, it behoves Europe to preserve with holy care the specimens that remain. The churches of this species which, for technical skill, very far surpass the most celebrated structures of Greece and Rome,* were constructed from the middle of the thirteenth to the end of the fourteenth century ; at which latter period the style had become debased by decorations which, in many examples, and especially in that of the minster at Ulm, evidently announce the period of its decay. In the sixteenth century it was no more.

The revival of the arts in Italy, induced by the commerce and riches of that country, brought in a very different style of architecture, namely, that of the Italian school, which has lasted throughout Europe to the present period, and is likely to endure until some general change in the habits of its different nations shall render necessary, or justify, some other style as its successor—as has been seen in the preceding section.

Such is a very short view of the early architec-

* It is a curious fact that the science of arch building, practically, seems to have retrograded, as the philosophical principles of equilibrium have become more scientifically known.

ture of the Germans, among whose professors are en-
rolled the illustrious names of Erwin of Steinbach,
and Stültz of Cologne. Even Italy, for architectural assistance, was indebted to the Germans; for
Vasari says, that Lapo, a German architect, was
employed in the early parts of Sta. Maria del Fiore,
at Florence, though Milizia seems to deny it: and it
is well authenticated, that Zamodia, a German, Annex
of Friburg, and Ulric of Ulm, were engaged on the
cathedral at Milan. Franchetti† says, the first of
these was employed about 1391, the period of the
golden age of pointed architecture in Germany.
The French contest the claim of the Germans to
the invention of pointed architecture, but, as it appears
to me, without sufficient grounds; indeed, the reputation of the Germans at the time was so great, that
John and Simon of Cologne, were engaged to build
the cathedral at Burgos in Spain.

From the revival of the arts, to nearly the end of
the eighteenth century, Germany furnishes the names
of but few architects who are known beyond the limits
of that country. During that period Italy seems to
have furnished them with several. Carlo Fontana was
engaged on works at Fulda and Vienna; Guarini on
the church of Sta. Anna at Prague; Scammozi on the
cathedral at Salzburg; Andrea Pozzo on several
churches in Vienna, where he died; besides others,
whom it is not necessary to enumerate: so that Italy
had the means of repaying, in kind, the debt which

* Storia e Descrizione del Duomo di Milano. 4to. Milano, 1821.

it formerly had contracted, to the German architects. Besides these, the French architects found their
way into the country, for it is well known that Blon-
del was extensively engaged throughout Germany towards the end of the 17th century.   Pietro Cart, who
built the bridge at Nuremberg, Neuman and Bott,
and Eosander of Prussia, are the only architects of the
period recorded by Milizia.   But, however, whoso
were the architects of the buildings of this time, the
designs of them seem to follow the style of those of
parallel periods in France, even down to the bizarreries of the time of Louis XV., rather than the some-
what more purified styles which were contemporaneous in Italy ; and it is a curious fact, that at the
period when Germany was borrowing architects from
France, and the last named country, England could
boast of architects whose fame still resounds through
Europe.

During the last fifty or sixty years, the Germans
have, however, produced some clever men ; among
whom must be noticed Weinbrenner, who may indeed
be called the modern father of the art in Germany.
My business is not, however, to give any farther account of German architecture than is above placed
before the reader, the object of this section being that
of noticing the works of the two most celebrated artists
of the country, whom the reviewer, before quoted, has
set up evidently with the view of instituting an in-
sidious comparison between them and the architects
of his own country, making them not only the idols of

his worship, but endeavouring to induce the English public also to fall down and worship them.

It is an exceedingly unpleasant task for an artist at any time to criticise the works of his cotemporaries, more especially is it so in the case of foreign artists. I have no doubt of the sincerity of the reviewer in his admiration of the works of Schinkel, Klenze, and Möller, and had that been confined to his own circle, nobody could have had the right or desire to interfere; but when a person attempts to lead the taste of the public—when he thinks his sentiments of sufficient importance for general promulgation—when he delivers his judgment as it were *ex cathedrâ*, it becomes the duty of those who understand the subject better than himself to step forward and remove the film with which he would unwittingly dim the eyes of the multitude. As that which a man writes on any subject is the best criterion for ascertaining his knowledge about it, the sufficiency or insufficiency of a reviewer is very easily detected by the few; and it is from such a test I must pronounce that our reviewer's information on the subject whereof he writes is far too small to justify the bold undertaking he attempted. I must here beg to declare that it is not with the view of disparaging the German architects in the eyes of my countrymen that I have volunteered these pages; no one can have a higher respect for the talents of German artists generally than myself; but it is to prevent young students and amateurs considering the works on which the following strictures are offered as models of imitation, as the reviewer would make them. Among the eminent men of the country in question is Möller, who has done more for the perfect knowledge and illustration of Gothic architecture, than all the writers together who have preceded him. The reviewer's remarks on the works of this artist will be the subject of some criticism. I therefore think it proper here to state the value in which I hold the service he has rendered the public; and, first in his case, to shew the reader how injudicious the reviewer is * in his selections, and how he has singled out what I have no hesitation in calling Möller's worst work, and one, moreover, which is unfinished.

The reviewer commences his operations by a quotation from Carl Menzel, which, though it contain nothing new, may as well be inserted here, as, from an equal belief with him in the doctrine of that writer, he and I arrive at very opposite conclusions. † "No work of art can ever be produced by skill and understanding alone, but *the inspiration of the artist ever has been, and ever must be, the source of that which confers æsthetic value on his productions.* A piece of architecture, in which there are any manifestations of genius, is worked out in the same manner as a poem. Invention, or the ground idea of the subject, must come first, and it is to this conception of the fancy that technical skill is afterwards to be applied, so as to

* Foreign Quarterly, No. XXVII., p. 98.

† This is, I suppose, the reviewer's translation; which I adopt, as the original work is not now before me.

work it up, and to render practicable in construction what is originally the mere apprehension of beauty. *This is the only true process* : by adopting the opposite course we may, indeed, be able to obtain a structure in every respect well suited to its destination; but it can never possess that mysterious charm which genius alone can bestow, nor will it ever warm the beholder to admiration, although he may not be able to deny that the builder has performed all that utility requires, or that mere reason ought to demand."

The first design which the reviewer has selected for his eulogy is Möller's circular church at Darmstadt, of which he thus speaks : " The Catholic church at Darmstadt is a rotunda, whose internal diameter measures one hundred and sixty-four Darmstadt feet,* and is *avowedly formed upon the plan of the Pantheon at Rome*, being lighted, like that, by a single aperture in the centre of the dome, and the height to the summit of the latter being equal to the diameter within the peristyle, viz., one hundred and thirty-two feet. The dome itself, however, bears a much greater proportion to its tambour (or cylindrical part of the edifice), the height to the top of the cornice being barely sixty feet." It appears, from his account, that it was the architect's aim to preserve all the essential beauties which characterise the interior of the Roman structure, and to avoid that multiplicity and minuteness of parts, together with other defects, which impair its grandeur, and detract from the harmony of the

* 135 English feet. The inner diameter of the Pantheon is 137½ feet.

whole; nor can it be denied that he has greatly sim-
plified his building by substituting for the unequal
graces, the numerous recesses, and the double tier of
ordinances " (orders I suppose) "in the original, a
continuous peristyle of twenty-eight insulated columns,
upon whose entablature the *vault*" (dome must be
meant) "rests."   By the subjoined diagram this

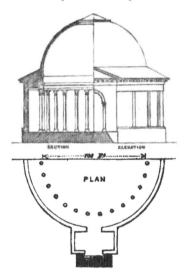

description will be better understood.   Now, any
person who reads the preceding quotation would be
naturally led to infer that Darmstadt really possessed an edifice which had reasonable claims to be
ranked as a rival of the Roman Pantheon, and that
the Catholic church was a building with a stone *vault*,
as the reviewer calls the dome.   What then will
be his surprise on the discovery that this noble
vault is of carpentry, and nineteen feet less than

G

the old *Halle aux bleds* at Paris! In plan it has
just as much resemblance to the Pantheon as the
latter has to any other circular building in the
world. The coffers of the dome, instead of being
bold sinkings, are painted in relief, thus impart-
ing to it a poverty even to meanness, which without
a survey of the thing itself can scarcely be conceived. The order of the peristyle is profiled in a
very singular manner—one quite unknown, I believe, in
any previous example, either antient or modern; for
instance, in the bed moulding of the cornice there is a
fillet, between the modillion band and the eggs, which
fillet projects before the band itself; and the bead of
the lower facia of the architrave projects before the
face of the upper facia. If these be some of the
happy innovations and deviations that the reviewer
thinks an architect entitled to make, in order to escape
from the bondage of technical rules, which none of his
class from want of comprehension approve, I hereby
beg him to excuse me in entering a formal protest
against all such fantastic tricks, as contrary to all
sound building and analogy, in whatsoever the type
be placed. The student must pass by and turn away
from them as abuses of intolerable impurity.

But to return to the comparison with the Pantheon, which with this lath and plaster building I have
scarcely patience to do. I cannot suppose that it was
the reviewer's intention to mislead either in matter of
fact or opinion, as far as he was capable of forming a
judgment; but it is necessary to say something ex-

planatory of the description I have above quoted. The
diameter of the Darmstadt dome is twenty-seven feet
less than the diameter between the external walls,
that is, by twice the width of the ambulatory between
them and the peristyle ; so that, instead of the proportion of 135 feet to 137½*, the diameter of the brick
dome of the Pantheon, the timber dome of the Catholic
church is only 108 feet in diameter, or thereabouts,
being fifteen feet less than that of the Colosseum in the
Regent's Park.   Of the comparative beauty of the
Darmstadt and the Roman buildings, it would be
absurd to waste a word.   In point of workmanship,
as in all the German buildings, it is astonishing to
any Englishman, who has observed the excellent mode
in which his countrymen turn out their work, to notice the great inferiority as to mere manufacture in
which the foreign artisan executes his task, whether
it be in the mason's, in the carpenter's, or in any other
department.   In this country, the execution which is
there admired would not be tolerated.   The exterior
of the building in question is not yet finished, or, as
the reviewer says, "it is *in a provisional state ;*" but
its general form and proportions are such, that it never
can be brought into competition with the Colosseum
in the Regent's Park, either in design or effect.
Having so condemned the church at Darmstadt, I
turn with much pleasure to a more important work,
which M. Möller is now superintending, namely, the
restoration of the cathedral at Mayence—an operation

* The diameter is nearer to 140 feet.

which he is carrying forward in so admirable a manner, and with so consummate a knowledge of the
subject, that I do not hesitate to say, his equal is not
to be found in 'Europe, and that if in this species his
designs be equal to his knowledge, and the times for
such a purpose were not out of joint, he is the architect
that could reintroduce the pointed style of architecture. It is far from my purpose to follow the reviewer
in offering observations on the works of Langhans,
Knobelsdorff, Boumann, Goutard, and others. The
celebrated work of the first named, the Brandenburg
Gate at Berlin, is little less than a copy of the propylæa
at Athens, and as I think all copies, whether of ancient
or modern art, prove a sad poverty of imagination on
the part of the copying artist, it is unnecessary to detain
the reader by any remarks on it : such examples do not
entitle a person to the appellation of an architect.
The rest, and others not named, have doubtless produced works of considerable merit; but our business
now is with the museum at Berlin, to which the
reader's attention is directed. This museum, which
is for the reception of pictures and sculpture, " is
divided," according to the description of the reviewer,
" into a low basement, and two upper floors, whose windows appear on three of its sides; and it forms a regular
unbroken *oblong* of two hundred and seventy-six feet,
by one hundred and seventy. The principal façade,
which is on one of the longer sides, namely, that
towards the south, consists entirely of a grand colonnade of nineteen intercolumns, formed by eighteen

fluted Ionic pillars forty feet high, and two very broad
antæ at the angles.   These columns rest upon a solid
stylobate of the same height as the basement story in
the other fronts, and unbroken, save by the flight of
steps in the centre, which occupies the width of seven
intercolumns, and their pillars.   Within the portico,
this central portion has five open intercolumns, and
their pillars (i. e., four columns in antis), beyond
which is a low screen with open work bronze doors,
enclosing the staircase, whose upper part, thus thrown
into perspective, contributes in no small degree to the
picturesque magnificence of this architectural scene.
Neither are the other parts of the *back ground* to
the *colonnade* less remarkable for the taste and richness they display; for the wall, on either side of this
receding division, is embellished through its whole
extent, by *enriched fascias*, and OTHER *ornamental*
MOULDINGS, and numerous compartments, inlaid with
variegated marbles, besides a series of reliefs, while
the whole upper part of each wall is intended to be
filled with a large painting in fresco."   Here follows
an apostrophe from the reviewer, with which, as there
is a small plan, section, and elevation of the building
in question on the following page, I request the
reader, as he peruses it, to compare with the thing
itself.   The passage accompanies the description just
quoted, thus :—

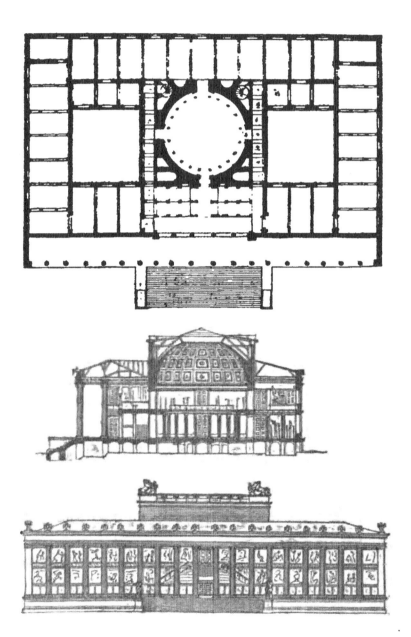

" Here let us pause, and ask if there be any other
modern work of architecture to be paralleled with this,
when all its decorations shall have been completed?
*What simplicity of outline, yet what variety and origi-
nality in the design ! What classical feeling, combined
with NOVEL invention !   What exuberant pomp, yet
what refined chastity of style ! Here the great German
master has conceived an edifice worthy to be a palace of the arts, liberal, but not profuse; he has arrayed
it both in loveliness and splendour, and has shed
around it the halo of a poetic imagination.*"   Did the
reader, as applied to the building placed before him,
ever read such a farrago of stilted and bombastic non-
sense as is strung together in this effusion? Simplicity
of outline, of course, means the long parallelogrammatic
front, without a break to relieve its monotony, with
the poverty of a single rank of columns, and the ceiling
they support to produce shadow on the wall behind
them.   The crowning member is frittered by a row of
eagles, perhaps allusive to the heraldic Prussian eagle ;
or if not, without meaning, but if properly allusive to
it, very injudiciously introduced.   Lest I forget, before turning to any thing else, I recommend the reader
to observe how sadly the unity of the design is broken
by the architect showing the spectator that the order,
which he would naturally suspect answered to a single
story inside, is cut into two, by the staircase, which
the reviewer considers so great a beauty, but which,
according to all notions of propriety in art, is a defect
of the first order, and of which I do not think another

example can be found, nor is this likely ever to be
followed as a model. It is, perhaps, one of the reviewer's "novel inventions," or perhaps the "variety
and originality" wherewith the reviewer advises the
student to finish his studies. It is easy to conceive
how a person unacquainted with the first principles of
architecture, which the reviewer evidently is, may have
his eye dazzled and carried away by a colonnade of so
great an extent; but the eye of the educated architect
is not satisfied with a meagre display of this sort.
The want of variety, and of light and shade consequent, renders the mass uninteresting; it has no
feature; all is sameness. The "*exuberant pomp*" I
am unable to discover, nor in what manner the great
German master, as the reviewer calls him, "*has shed
around it the halo of a poetic imagination.*" I hope
the reader may be able to do so. To me it seems more
like the composition of a scene painter, than of an architect, and that the reviewer's encomiums are mere
verbiage. Still this building is in far better taste than
the Glyptothek at Munich, which I have hereafter to
notice. The reviewer is enchanted with the concealment of the dome, but the fact is, that this very
concealment shows how the façade had so run away
with all the architect's thoughts, that he could not, or
would not, combine the plan and section with the elevation, and was thus obliged to use a mask to hide a
defect he had created. This, which is a defect, the
reviewer then discovers to be a beauty. "The rotunda
itself," he continues, "which divides the inner area

into two distinct courts, is sixty-seven feet in diameter, by seventy in height, and the lower part is surrounded by a peristyle of twenty fluted columns with foliaged capitals of Grecian design.   Above this peristyle runs a gallery communicating with the apartments on the upper floor.   The rooms on the lower floor contain the collection of sculpture and other antiquities ; and the principle ones are a large gallery upwards of two hundred feet in length, and two lesser ones one hundred and twenty-three feet each.   The first of these is thirty feet wide, the others twenty-nine; and they are all divided into three equal portions or aisles by two rows of Doric columns,—the same we have already noticed for the singular beauty of their decorated capitals.   Above these are picture galleries of the same extent, on the upper floor ; but these are partitioned off by cross screens extending from the piers between the windows, so as to form a series of cabinets, viz., eleven in the longer, and seven in each of the shorter galleries." Upon examining the section of this building, the reader will be immediately struck by the mode in which an otherwise well proportioned circular salon is cut up.   One fault always entails another : the subdivision of this salon into two stories by the peristyle and gallery thereover has spoilt all the effect of the dome internally, and was the cause of the staircase under the portico which I have before objected to.   I do not mean to go into minor details, or I should object to the doors in the gallery of the peristyle running up to the underside of the entablature,

and to the bases and capitals, which are unpleasing in
profile. From this edifice, not less than that of the
Glyptothek at Munich, it is manifest that the German
is founded on the French school, very far behind which
it however ranks; the beauties of the latter being over-
looked or misunderstood, while its defects and abuses
are pertinaciously preserved. The practice of cutting
through stylobatæ by doors, which is not only a viola-
tion of all propriety, but exceedingly destructive of
effect, by breaking lines, is constantly resorted to by the
German architects.

It is rather extraordinary that in a country like
Germany, in which finer specimens of pointed architecture are to be seen than elsewhere in Europe, the
architects generally have not imbibed the feeling of,
nor have they been able to imitate, that style. Schinkel's attempts in it are altogether worthless, and if
possible even worse than the Gothic of Batty Langley,
now almost forgotten. The reviewer, however, allows
that the church in the Werdersche Markte, "although
for the *most part* in conformity with the pointed style,
exhibits also *considerable deviations from it*, as in the
doors of the portal, and the deep acanthus cornice
beneath the parapet, besides many others in the lesser
details." The truth really is, that in this country
Schinkel's designs for Gothic would not be tolerated
for an instant. So little are the principles and peculiarities of the style understood by him, that there is
scarcely an architect's office which could not produce
pupils of two or three years standing far his superiors.

Schinkel is, nevertheless, an artist of great merit, not-withstanding the defects of which we have been speaking; but when compared with the French architects, and many of the English ones, he must be content to hold a subordinate place among them. Compared with the façade of Mr. Cockerell's chapel in Regent Street, there is not a building by either Klenze, or Schinkel, worth notice, either for design or execution. Architectural works of great magnitude rarely occur in this country; but when they do, jobbing for patronage immediately begins : witness the late instance—the National Gallery, which is, as was predicted, now universally condemned.

I now come to the reviewer's notions on the works of Klenze, an artist very inferior to him of whom I have just been speaking. His principal works are the Glyptothek, of which I have given a reduced representation on the following page, and the Pinacothek at Munich, the former being the sculpture, and the latter the picture gallery. " The Glyptothek," says the reviewer, " is an insulated building about two hundred and twenty feet square, with a court in its centre, and without any windows externally, except two large ones in the back front, the different apartments being lighted, either by domes or spacious windows towards the court, formed in the arches of the vaulted ceilings. By this means the architect has got rid of many difficulties in point of design, while, there being only a single floor, and the windows raised nearly to the top of the building, sufficient light is ob-

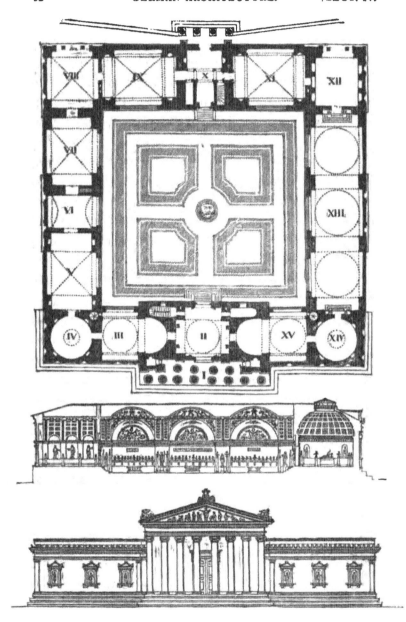

tained, because the court is so spacious in proportion
to the height of the edifice, that the opposite side
cannot be seen from within. The *style* '(*order*)' adopted
for the exterior is Ionic, in a certain degree modified
according to the architect's own ideas, yet still decidedly
Grecian in character. The principal façade has an octastyle portico, advancing one column, before the general
line of the front, and recessed about as much within
it, and these two divisions of it are separated by an
inner range of four columns, forming five open intercolumns, those at the extremities being between antæ.
The effect of this portico, which is raised on three *exceedingly deep steps*, is very imposing and classical,
owing to the narrowness of the intercolumns, as well
as to the *multiplicity* of the columns themselves, and
the great depth of shade thus produced." The columns
are not fluted, which occasions the reviewer to re-
mark, that although *he* considers *flutings to columns
to be almost indispensable for their* 'full beauty,' he
does not object to their absence in the Glyptothek,
albeit their "neckings are sculptured." But I must
continue the writer's description of the building.—
"The lateral divisions of this elevation are not so
lofty as the portico itself, the podium by which they
are surmounted rising no higher than the moulding
beneath the necking of the Ionic columns. These
parts, therefore, assume the appearance of low wings,
attached to a centre, whose roof is seen to extend, in
continuation of the pediment, the whole depth of the
building as far as the inner court." The wings, as

the reader will see by reference to the plate, are
flanked by antæ, between which are what the reviewer
calls, three "large tabernacle niches," with Greek
antefixæ, "coming against the lower part of the upper
podium." Before proceeding to the rest of the design,
I shall offer a few observations on what has been de-
scribed. The façade consists, as we have seen, of
three parts, the portico and its wings, or whatever
other name they may bear. Now let the reader
look at the plate, and ascertain whether, in style, proportion, or subordination, they have the slightest relation
to each other; nay, more, whether the two wings
would not suit as appendages to the National Gallery
at Charing Cross, or any other building in the world,
as well as they do to the octastyle portico of the Glyptothek at Munich. Nobody could believe they be-
longed to the building whereto they are attached, unless favoured with a sight of the plan. The antefixæ
which range above them do not perform their real
office, that of hiding the joints of tiles, or other covering, and are, therefore, ornaments misplaced, and the
very podium that backs them thence makes their
adoption the more absurd. If the Greeks had played
fantastic tricks of this sort, we should not still continue
to hold their works in veneration. The " tabernacle
niches " one might suppose to have been borrowed
from some such building as Diocletian's palace at
Spalatro, and decked out with Greek foliage on their
pediments. I fear not all that all the reviewers in the
world can say, when I pronounce them to be in a most

barbarous taste ; they are, moreover, so inordinately large, that, even if they had been much purer than they are, they completely overpower and destroy the magnitude of the portico. The Ionic of the portico, which we are told, is "modified according to the architect's own ideas," is a matter more for a man's personal taste, and therefore, whatever my own opinion of it may be, I shall not detain the reader upon it further than to observe, that I think it indifferently profiled : so do I say nothing on the reviewer's fancy about the indispensability of flutings for the *full beauty* of columns, except that he seems very uninformed on the first principles of the art, when he says, he thinks the architect might have left their shafts plain, "to give them such a breadth of effect as should cause them to harmonize with other parts of the façade, and also to avoid the *confusion* that might have been produced by so many perpendicular lines, the columns themselves being very closely set, and there being another range behind the first." Now, the reviewer may be assured that M. Klenze could have had no such reason as the reviewer assigns for the omission, inasmuch as vertical and horizontal objects cannot be injured in breadth by subdivisions in the same directions ; but angular and circular subdivisions will destroy breadth. The opinion on the "exceedingly deep steps" of the portico I consider, as I am sure the reader also will, another absurdity of the writer. Steps are made for ascent, and they are only proper and beautiful as the ascent they afford is easy. There are certain things whose magnitudes and proportions cannot be altered, as Hogarth has well explained in his analysis of beauty.   On reference to the plan and section it will be seen that the arrangement of this edifice is that of a series of camerated apartments surrounding a quadrangle ; those on the left hand side, on entering, are in their three middle bays so like the section in plate 13, of the second part of Durand's Leçons d'Architecture, that one would almost suppose it was copied from it.   With some critics a doubt might exist how far the interior and exterior of a building should necessarily correspond with each other.   In the Glyptothek there is not the slightest correspondence between the external and internal architecture ; the first aims at being Grecian, the last is founded on the forms, and arrangement, and vaultings of a Roman bath ; for it is in this that we find the series of camerated chambers that are the prototypes of this sculpture gallery. This species has been the favorite of the French school, in all their designs, for the last half century; and to these, both in design and decoration, M. Von Klenze is evidently very much indebted.   The reviewer seems captivated with the halls and galleries, which, he says, " are remarkable for their architectural luxury, which gradually increases in splendour ; since, although a sufficient uniformity of style is observed throughout, in the particular mode of embellishment and the ornaments, regard has been had, as far as possible, to the particular character of the subjects to which each is respectively appropriated :" and again,

" all the rooms have inlaid marble pavements, and, in-
dependently of the variety and richness of their vaulted
roofs, and their cornices, acquire no small splendour
from different coloured stuccos and marbles with which
their walls are coated," &c.   That there is taste in
the decoration is quite true, but, as every architect
knows, all this is an easy affair, compared with the
general forms which are the test of an architect's skill.
Upon the whole, then, I can by no means agree with
the reviewer, that the Glyptothek, when completed,
will " be one of the proudest and completest works of
modern times."   So far from that being the case, I
have no hesitation in pronouncing the Pinacothek, in
the same city, and by the same artist, infinitely superior to it in every respect.   In the Pinacothek the
effect is, however, more the result of the repetition of
the parts than of beautiful and nicely balanced features.   The stylobate, with its plinths and different
sorts of ashlers, is in rather barbarous taste, and the
mode of bringing the doors down through it, highly
objectionable.   The antefixæ have no business in
their places, and the circular windows, in square

headed dressings, are very
badly composed.   The general form of plan of this
building is here given, it
is 500 feet long and 90 feet wide, with 170 feet of
façade to the ends, and necessarily a very imposing
structure ; and, being designed more in the style of
the Venetian school, seems better suited to the age and

H

country for whose use it is erected. " The elevations are all very similar, and exhibit a basement of *lofty proportions*, with a bold rustic course," which is above reprobated, "beneath the windows, and very massive rustic quoins of the same kind at the angles. The windows and doors are," as I have already said, in very bad taste, "arched, but all enclosed within square framing, the spandrils being filled up with carving ; above this basement rises an attached Ionic order continued quite round the building, with a rich console frieze. The intercolumns are occupied by very large arcade windows, on whose keystones the architrave rests, so as to occasion a great superficies of aperture, such as would give this upper structure an air of too great lightness, were it not counteracted," a thing which was never dreamt of by the architect, "by the solidity of the projecting part of the wings." The reviewer, then, allows that, though he is by no means an admirer of the Italian school, he must admit that an edifice like this is almost sufficient to overcome his prejudices against it. In short, he seems to approve of his favorite German masters in all they do.

I now take my leave of the German school and its encomiast. That it will improve I have no doubt, at present it is neither Italian nor Greek, but rather a bad compound of both, and no more to be compared with the French school, than are the compositions of the Italian painters of the present age, with the beautiful and affecting designs of that honor to Germany and to the art of Europe, MORITZ RETSCH.

DRURY, PRINTER, JOHNSON'S COURT, FLEET STREET.

CPSIA information can be obtained at www.ICGtesting.com
Printed in the USA
BVOW08s1031140714

359105BV00035B/1531/P